Advance Praise for:

HOW TO SURVIVE YOUR BABY'S FIRST YEAR

"The HUNDREDS OF HEADS folks have done it again! *How To Survive Your Baby's First Year* is a terrific compendium of baby advice from the best experts you'll never meet. Literally hundreds of moms and dads from all over offer their nuggets of wisdom—some sweet, some funny, all smart—on giving birth, coming home and bringing up baby."

—*ANDREA SARVADY*
AUTHOR OF BABY GAMI

"*How to Survive Your Baby's First Year* functions as a powerful support group that gives you a wide range of different perspectives and experiences. When you need encouragement, feel insecure about your parenting, or just want some handy tips from other parents, this book will be your indispensable guide."

—*CYNTHIA BOMAN THOMPSON*
FREELANCE WRITER AND MOTHER OF TWO BOYS (13 AND 11)

"Not only for parents, a must read for doctors too, providing insights into parental concerns not ordinarily addressed in their basic medical education."

—*JOSEF SOLOWAY, M.D., F.A.A.P.*
CLINICAL ASSOCIATE PROFESSOR OF PEDIATRICS
WEILL MEDICAL COLLEGE OF CORNELL UNIVERSITY

Praise for other HUNDREDS OF HEADS™ *guides:*

HOW TO SURVIVE DATING

"I'm not a fan of the so-called experts. What do they know? This is the first book (and series) that gives it to you straight from real people who have been there in the trenches. Unlike so many other self-help books, I actually read this one."

—*Steve Linowes*
Washington, DC

"A great handbook to one of life's best adventures. HUNDREDS OF HEADS sharing their wisdom. Practical, readable and fun."

—*J.R. Williamson*
Atlanta, Georgia

"I couldn't put it down. The stories and advice are hilarious and wise. I can't wait to try some of this in the real world."

—*Leslie Kimerling*
New York, New York

HOW TO SURVIVE YOUR FRESHMAN YEAR

"An amazing collection of tips, stories and fun. A tour de force. A great send-off for every high school senior."

—*Jeffrey P. Kahn, Ph.D*
Professor, University of Minnesota, Director, Center for Bioethics

"If only there had been a guide like this when I went to college, I could have avoided a lot of mistakes."

—*Leslie Gilbert-Lurie*
President, Los Angeles County Board of Education

How to
Survive
Your
BABY's
First Year

WARNING:

This Guide contains differing opinions. Hundreds of Heads will not always agree. Advice taken in combination may cause unwanted side effects. Use your Head when selecting advice.

How to Survive Your

's First Year

by Hundreds of Happy Parents Who Did*

*and some things to avoid, from a few who barely made it™

edited by
LORI BANOV KAUFMANN AND YADIN KAUFMANN
with JAMIE ALLEN

Hundreds of Heads Books, Inc.
ATLANTA

Library of Congress Library of Congress
Cataloging in Publication Division CIP 20540-4320
101 Independence Avenue, S.E. 9140 East Hampton Drive
Washington, DC 20540-4320 Capitol Heights, MD 20743
See page 239 for credits and permissions.

Cover and book design by Elizabeth Johnsboen

Cover photograph by Image Source
Interior illustrations by Image Club

HUNDREDS OF HEADS™ books are available at special discounts when purchased in bulk for premiums or institutional or educational use. Excerpts and custom editions can be created for specific uses. For more information, please email sales@hundredsofheads.com or write to:

HUNDREDS OF HEADS BOOKS, INC.
#230
2221 Peachtree Road, Suite D
Atlanta, GA 30309

ISBN 0-9746292-2-7

Printed in U.S.A.
10 9 8 7 6 5 4 3 2 1

CONTENTS

Introduction

This book, the third in the HUNDREDS OF HEADS™ Survival Guide series, grew out of the simple idea that when you're facing any of life's major challenges—such as being responsible for another human being when you can barely find matching socks— it's good to get advice from people who have "been there, done that." Why not learn from others' mistakes?

Other advice books, no matter how smart or expert their authors, are generally limited to the knowledge of only one person. This book takes a different approach: It assembles the experiences of hundreds of people, scarred veterans of the diaper wars who, having traveled that road, have emerged with some wisdom to share. If two heads are better than one, as the saying goes, then hundreds of them are even better.

To create this book, we interviewed moms and dads from all over the country (and even a few from around the world). What they told us about their parenting experiences was remarkably universal. It confirmed that all of us encounter similar challenges, and that we all do quite a bit of winging it, fumbling around, and improvising. Luckily, though, those little creatures are quite sturdy and seem to thrive in spite of us.

As you might expect, we heard many different views—and you'll often find opposite views on the same aspects of parenting. You may not agree with a particular respondent's point of view, but in this book you can choose from hundreds of others. So read on. Armed with the wisdom of all these people, you may make fewer mistakes yourself and have more fun along the way.

You will survive your baby's first year, trust us. It's the teenage phase that will do you in.

Lori Banov Kaufmann
Yadin Kaufmann

SPECIAL THANKS

Thanks to our intrepid "headhunters" for going out to find so many parents from around the country with interesting advice to share:

Jamie Allen, Chief Headhunter

Jennifer Blaise
Scott Deckman
Elizabeth Edwardsen
Sara Faiwell
Shannon Hurd
Teena Hammond
Lisa Jaffe Hubbell
Natasha Lambropoulos
Nicole Lessin
R.M. Lofton
Ken McCarthy
Lindsey Roth Miller
Jennifer Nittoso
Christina Orlovsky
Adam Pollock
Peter Ramirez
William Ramsey
Kazz Regelman
Jennifer Bright Reich
Dana Rothblatt
Beth Turney Rutchik
Graciela Sholander
Laura Roe Stevens
Jade Walker
Sara Walker
Wendy Webb
Jennifer Weiner

Thanks, too, to our editorial advisors Anne Kostick and Francine Almash. And thanks to our assistant, Miri Greidi, for yeoman's work keeping us all organized.

The real credit for this book, of course, goes to all the people whose experiences and collective wisdom make up this guide. There are too many of you to thank individually, of course, but you know who you are. Thanks for sharing.

LITTLE HEADS

So you'll know just how expert our parent-respondents really are, we've included their credentials in this book. Look for these icons:

= A son
= A daughter
- = Twins
= Pregnant

Numeral = age in years except:
M = Months
W = Weeks
D = Days

1 Pregnancy: Let the Journey Begin

The stars aligned, the arrow hits its mark and one tough swimmer beat the pack—in other words, you're pregnant! Congratulations! Now what? Oh boy. Or girl . . . There's a lot to know, a lot to worry about, and a lot to NOT worry about. Did you ever conceive there could be so much information? Welcome to a whole new world.

THE THREE MOST IMPORTANT THINGS TO DO when you're pregnant: Read, read, and read! Read lots of books and magazines about other people's experiences with parenthood. Even if they contradict each other, you'll get a more complete picture of life with baby.

—*M.S.L.*
WAIKOLOA, HAWAII
40 37

A LOT OF PREGNANCY IS ABOUT SLOWING DOWN.

—*PATTY*
LOS ANGELES, CALIFORNIA
2

Sleep, read lots of books, save up as much money as you can, get the necessary baby items (diapers, bottles, etc.), and take Lamaze classes.

—*E. Hirsh*
West Palm Beach, Florida
7

When you're pregnant, make sure you have a great relationship with your gynecologist. This person will see more of you than your spouse.

—*Kerri*
Marietta, Georgia
4 2

I found a good doctor before I got pregnant. I started by asking people for recommendations, then I called the doctor's office and asked questions like: Where is the doctor's hospital affiliation? How long is the wait for appointments? What is their Caesarean section rate? After that I toured different hospitals before making my choice.

—*Della D.*
Bridgeport, New York
15 9 -8 1

I really got into this business about "eating for two"—it sounded like a great excuse to eat whatever I wanted, whenever I wanted. After all, I had to make sure the baby was getting enough nutrition. At some point, though, I realized that one of the people I was supposedly eating for was the size of a peanut—so I decided I had better cut back!

—*Lori B.*
Charleston, South Carolina
19 16 13 3

In the mornings, I would watch my husband put on his suit, and I'd look at myself under the covers and feel like a giant blimp. I'd have these irrational thoughts like, "Why isn't he the one who's fat like this?"

—*Loraine*
Boston, Massachusetts
38 35

THINK ABOUT HAVING YOUR BABY SHOWER after your baby is born. I was superstitious about having the shower before I'd delivered, so my shower was held when my baby was six weeks old. She came with me and all my friends got to see her. Other benefits—we knew what sex she was and how big she was.

—*ELIZABETH EDWARDSEN*
SOUTH PORTLAND, MAINE
7

"Don't listen to other people's pregnancy horror stories, because the experience is different for everyone."

—*WENDI K.*
PARKER, COLORADO
8 5

IN MY SIXTH MONTH, I began to think of myself as a Weeble! When I was sitting back on a couch, I had to push over to one side and roll myself up. It was so much more of an effort to get from sitting to standing.

—*LAUREL*
SAN FRANCISCO, CALIFORNIA
1

Grin and bear it. It's only nine months.

—*VERONICA*
CARTAGENA, COLOMBIA
4

I LOVED EVERY MINUTE OF BEING PREGNANT. I got so much attention from everybody. Random strangers were always rubbing my belly. Plus, I liked having my daughter in there safe.

—*SAMANTHA BESSEMER*
SAN ANTONIO, TEXAS
2M

NO WAY TO START A DAY

PREPARE TO THROW UP. A LOT. Way more than you ever have in your entire life. Everyone will tell you to "eat crackers" but this will just make you associate "crackers" with throwing up.

—*LISA KRAMER*
NEW YORK, NEW YORK

• • • • • • • •

ONE OF THE ONLY WAYS TO SURVIVE THE HORROR of "morning sickness" (which, by the way, lasts all day) is to eat, sleep, eat and then eat some more. Sounds pretty good, right? Wrong! Eating helps relieve nausea only while in the process of chewing and for about five minutes after your last bite, and then it's back to doomsday. And it's almost impossible to find any foods that appeal to you in any way. Everything smells or sounds horrible! When you do find something appealing, you consistently eat that one thing for the next couple of days, until you can't stand the sight of it anymore.

—*KATE MOYNIHAN*
MINNEAPOLIS, MINNESOTA

• • • • • • • •

I DIDN'T EXPERIENCE NAUSEA until my most recent pregnancy. I opened up a can of Campbell's Chunky Soup for my husband, and it smelled like dog food to me. I ran straight to the bathroom.

—*DELLA D.*
BRIDGEPORT, NEW YORK
15 9 -8 1

• • • • • • • •

WITH MY FIRST PREGNANCY, THE NAUSEA LASTED FIVE MONTHS! I learned to get up slowly in the morning and drink lots of water. In later pregnancies, I kept unsalted crackers by the bed so that I could eat a little before actually getting up.

—*KATHARINE O'MOORE-KLOPF*
EAST SETAUKET, NEW YORK
21 9 2

WITH MY FIRST CHILD THE NAUSEA WAS SO AWFUL that I went to a boat store and bought a wristband that helps with seasickness. That gave me some relief. For my second pregnancy it was just as bad, but now I had a one-year-old to chase around the house, so I went straight to my doctor and he gave me a prescription.

—LISA
CHARLOTTE, NORTH CAROLINA
2 1

• • • • • • • •

FOR ME, MORNING SICKNESS WAS PSYCHOLOGICAL. I experienced nausea with my first pregnancy because people convinced me that getting sick was inevitable. But with my second pregnancy my mother said, "You probably won't get sick"—and I didn't. I believed her, and so I was OK.

—LINDA ANDREWS REEVES
SAN ANTONIO, TEXAS
10 5

• • • • • • • •

I HAD TO COMMUTE INTO NEW YORK CITY through morning sickness, a one-and-a-half hour journey each way. The only thing that got me through those weeks was a bagel with cream cheese on the way to work and then lying on the floor of my office until the nausea subsided.

—RACHEL LEON
CROTON-ON-HUDSON, NEW YORK
5 3

• • • • • • • •

FOR NAUSEA DURING PREGNANCY, eat gingersnap cookies and drink Coke.

—SHANNON L.
SAN RAFAEL, CALIFORNIA
16 15 13

WHILE MY BABIES WERE STILL IN MY TUMMY I spoke to them and sang to them. This is important. They feel the energy in the womb.

—*LEE*
PASSAIC, NEW JERSEY

I think every parent should be required to go to school to learn how to be a good parent.

—*BATIA ELKAYAM*
LOS ANGELES, CALIFORNIA

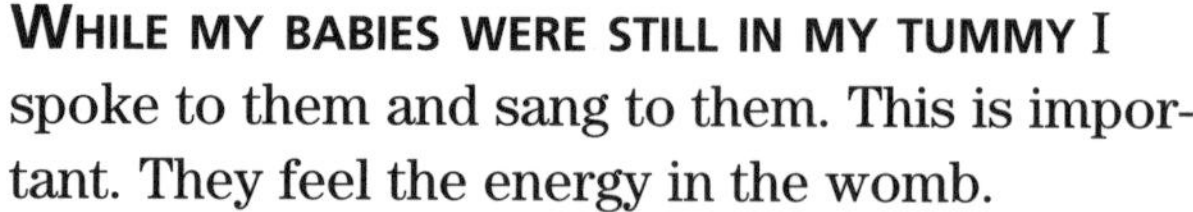

DON'T RUSH RIGHT OUT AND BUY maternity clothes when you're pregnant. Start out with a few inexpensive "regular" clothes that are stretchy or in bigger sizes. Save the maternity gear for when you really need it, because it adds up quickly!

—*J.D.*
BALTIMORE, MARYLAND
15 3

WHEN SHOPPING FOR MATERNITY CLOTHES, ask yourself, "Is this something I would wear even if I wasn't pregnant?" If the answer is no, then why would you think of putting it on your expecting figure?

—*ANONYMOUS*
SAN FRANCISCO, CALIFORNIA
2

EAT NORMAL, HEALTHY AMOUNTS and exercise while pregnant. I gained 40 pounds with my first child because I was excited to have a baby and I ate whatever I wanted. It took me nearly eight months to lose all the weight. During my other two pregnancies, I ate normal portions and worked out three to four times a week. After their births, I didn't have stretch marks or excess weight. I was in good shape.

—*ANONYMOUS*
CHICAGO, ILLINOIS
19 17 15

EVERYONE THINKS THEY HAVE TO GET the baby's room perfect before the child comes. The baby does not care what the room looks like. It's not going to affect how they sleep at night. Worry about getting more sleep and taking care of yourself before the baby comes. It's a better use of your time.

—*K.J.*
ST. AUGUSTINE, FLORIDA
6 1

• • • • • • • •

"I was constantly famished during my first pregnancy, and would wake up in the middle of the night to eat. I gained 65 pounds—I had stretch-marks on my hair!"

—*RACHEL DIAMOND CALOW*
WESTFORD, MASSACHUSETTS
9 7

• • • • • • • •

YOUR WIFE HAS TO TAKE CARE OF HER BODY and so should you. She can't have any alcohol, drugs, or cigarettes in her system. As a husband, it's your job to set the example and avoid the same things.

—*FLOYD CONDRON*
PARKER, COLORADO
32 31

Educate yourself. Read as much as possible, so that you can make informed choices.

—*TORI KOPPELMAA*
SAN JOSE, CALIFORNIA
6 -4 2

I USED TO LAY MY HEAD ON MY WIFE'S BELLY and say, "How ya doin' in there?" Sure, I risked an occasional kick in the head from a little foot, but right after both of the kids were born and I first held them, I said, "How ya doin'?" and they became quiet and calm. I like to think they recognized my voice.

—*R.A.*
CEDAR RAPIDS, IOWA
24 22

"One of the benefits of being pregnant is that people are very willing to help you."

—*INDIRA*
NEW YORK, NEW YORK
9M

DURING LAMAZE CLASS THE INSTRUCTOR told the men, "Tie a 10-pound bowling ball to your stomach and walk around for a couple of hours. You would be miserable."

—*CHUCK S.*
PONTE VEDRA BEACH, FLORIDA
9 4

IF YOU LIVE IN A HOT CLIMATE, the best way to ensure you get exercise is to go to the mall. They are always air conditioned.

—*L.E.*
TEMPE, ARIZONA
6 3

SAY CHEESE—AND SMILE!

Advice to people who work in drive-throughs: Never, ever cross a pregnant woman with a craving for cheese! When I was very pregnant, I was sitting in the drive-through line at Wendy's. It was at a standstill. I had been waiting for at least twenty minutes to place my order (unacceptable for a hungry, pregnant woman). All I wanted was a single with cheese—let me stress, *with cheese*—and a Frosty to dip my fries into. When I finally made it to the drive-through speaker I placed my simple, but oh-so-important order. They immediately informed me that the Frosty machine was broken—a tough blow, but I would make it. Another ten minutes went by while I waited for my food. And waited. And waited. I felt like I might pass out. Then, finally, order in hand, I made my way home. When I sat down at the table with my husband, I opened my burger . . . no cheese! How could this be? Didn't they know the importance of a pregnant woman's craving? How could they be so stupid? Slapping a piece of cheese on a burger is not a hard thing to do! The tears were uncontrollable. The words of utter defeat fell with them. My husband—my hero—immediately recognized the seriousness of the situation and ran to my rescue. "No one shall keep cheese from my beautiful, pregnant wife!" he shouted as he drove back to Wendy's. Face to face with the manager, hands on hips, he demanded cheese on my burger. The manager apologized meekly and quickly delivered a single with cheese. And then he said, "Please, for all your trouble, take this Frosty, free of charge." "But the Frosty machine is broken," my husband nearly said. Instead, he took the burger and shake and made his way home, victorious.

—M. Allen
Atlanta, Georgia
6 3

SHE'S GOTTA HAVE IT

I HAD INTENSE CRAVINGS FOR COCKTAIL ONIONS during my pregnancy. I could eat jars of them. One night at a party, my husband ordered me a martini, asking the bartender to "hold the martini" and give me a glassful of onions.

—K.H.
FAIRFAX, CALIFORNIA
5.5M

I ONCE ORDERED 11 LARGE FRIES FROM McDONALD'S, put them in a big bowl like popcorn, sat in front of soap operas and ate every last one of them.

—TINA M. COY
EL CAJON, CALIFORNIA
23 21

I CRAVED M&Ms, SO MY HUSBAND BOUGHT ME a one-pound bag. I ate them for a few nights in a row and saw it was becoming a trend, so I begged my husband to throw them away. I made him flush them down the toilet—like a drug addict!

—JEANNE-MARIE CROWE
FAIRFAX, CALIFORNIA
12W

I CRAVED ENTENMANN'S "POPPETTE" DONUTS. Before becoming pregnant, I would never have eaten them.

—DANA FARBER RAY
SAN FRANCISCO, CALIFORNIA
3W

I HAD CRAVINGS FOR TOMATO JUICE and beef jerky with my first child.

—T.D.
IOWA CITY, IOWA
31 28 25

I CRAVED—DON'T GAG—SAUERKRAUT AND PICKLED PIGS FEET. My poor husband watched me down a bowl of sauerkraut and a glass of skim milk for dinner every night. The night I brought out the jar of pickled pigs feet, he had to leave the table.

—Amy Rea
Eden Prairie, Minnesota
11 8

• • • • • • • •

ICE CREAM, RED MEAT, and eggs.

—Jessica Vaughan
Randolph, Vermont
10 8 6 4

• • • • • • • •

ONE DAY I CRAVED THE PICKLED GINGER that comes with sushi. The next I was on to mashed potatoes. It changed every day. I couldn't stand the smell of a supermarket, so my poor husband was left to call me from the store and suggest food groups.

—R.J.
Redmond, Washington
6

• • • • • • • •

I CRAVED DAIRY QUEEN BLIZZARDS. I had a coworker bring me back one every time he left the office.

—Kellye Crocker
Clive, Iowa
2

• • • • • • • •

ONE NIGHT I NEEDED BARBECUE RIBS. I went down to our local Irish pub, got myself a full rack to go, sat in front of the television, and ate them.

—Emily
Freeport, Maine
7 6

I don't have a lot of sympathy for people who say, "I'm tired because I'm pregnant." The entire time I was pregnant I delivered mail every day on a 14-mile route.

—*DEB S.*
SAN DIEGO, CALIFORNIA
21 13

WE DIDN'T HAVE ULTRASOUNDS when I had my kids, so when I was visiting my daughter during her second pregnancy, she and her husband invited me in to the appointment so I could have the experience. It took my breath away. Nobody who has the opportunity to see this should miss it.

—*LORAINE*
BOSTON, MASSACHUSETTS
38 35

• • • • • • • •

GO WITH YOUR WIFE TO THE ULTRASOUND appointments. They are the most fascinating thing to see—the first images of your baby, hearing the heartbeat, etc. Plus, your wife will kill you if you don't show up.

—*MARK KAPLAN*
FOSTER CITY, CALIFORNIA
3 1

My wife had one craving after another when she was pregnant, and I always tried to accommodate her. One night in December my wife woke me and said "I want banana cream pie!" I said, "Come on—I just fell asleep! There's snow up to the bottom of the windowsill! It's cold, windy, and miserable—can't you wait until tomorrow?" Reluctantly, she agreed, but she never did get the pie. When my daughter was born, there were four freckles on her lower back . . . forming a perfect banana. My Italian mother-in-law said the baby was "marred" because I wasn't a good husband.

Four years later, my wife was pregnant with our second child. One night in the eighth month, she said, "I'm dying for Chinese food." I got up, got dressed, and got Chinese food.

—*JOE SCOLES*
NEPTUNE, NEW JERSEY
54 51

I DIDN'T WANT THEM TO TELL ME if my baby was a boy or girl at the doctor's office. I asked them to write it down and put it in an envelope so my husband and I could go to dinner and open it together. It was more personal that way.

—*DELLA D.*
BRIDGEPORT, NEW YORK
15 9 -8 1

IN ORDER TO FEEL LIKE I WAS PART of the pregnancy, I decorated the nursery. It helped me mentally prepare for the baby. By setting aside time each day and working with my hands to paint canvases of our favorite cartoon and storybook characters for the baby, I could really reflect on what was happening.

—*TOM FISHBURNE*
MINNEAPOLIS, MINNESOTA
1

It was actually fun to see my husband gain sympathy weight. Men really do gain pounds with their wives!

—*ADRIANE*
FT. LAUDERDALE, FLORIDA
1

"When we told our three-year-old son that I was expecting another baby, and that he was going to have a little sister, he asked if he could go to the hospital with us and pick her out."

—*CONNIE*
LOS ANGELES, CALIFORNIA
3

SIX STEPS TO A PEACEFUL PREGNANCY

1. Tell your wife that she is beautiful, especially now that she has your baby inside her.

2. Don't make fun of her—even if she makes fun of you.

3. Expect lots of "wrong times." Hormones and psychology are raging and if you think PMS is bad you ain't seen nothin' yet.

4. Help her around the house.

5. Rub her feet (!)

6. Reassure, reassure, reassure—about EVERYTHING.

—*Kathy Penton*
Savannah, Georgia
23

I LIKE TO SLEEP ON MY STOMACH, and training myself to sleep on my side during my preganacy has been a challenge. I struggle, switching sides constantly. I feel like a beached whale!

—*JENNIFER SEILER*
SAN RAFAEL, CALIFORNIA

YOU DON'T HAVE TO BUY MATERNITY CLOTHES. A great pair of black elastic waist pants with some nice tops, and some stylish sweat suits can get you through.

—*T.N.*
HUNTINGTON BEACH, CALIFORNIA
19M 3.5M

"Sleep. Dear God, load up on all the sleep you can."

—*STEPHANIE WOLFE*
GROTON, CONNECTICUT
23M

BEFORE YOU HAVE A BABY, get your life in order. I was in the middle of a career change when my daughter arrived, and now, what might have taken me a year to accomplish will take me three.

—*DAN*
HELOTES, TEXAS
1.5

MAKE PLANS FOR FRIENDS and family members to run errands, cook meals, do housework, and field phone calls for at least two weeks after you give birth.

—*KATHARINE O'MOORE-KLOPF*
EAST SETAUKET, NEW YORK
21 9 2

The updated Velour sweat suit has revolutionized maternity clothes.

—*H.R.*
SAN FRANCISCO, CALIFORNIA
2

FOR DADS-TO-BE

WHEN SHE'S HAVING MOOD SWINGS, work late.

—*Tom Harris*
Waynesboro, Virginia
3 1

• • • • • • • •

THE HUSBAND HAS TO UNDERSTAND THAT WHEN HIS WIFE is pregnant she's going to be moody. Don't take it personally. Pregnancy requires a man to be a little more patient in the first three months. And even more patient in the last three months.

—*Tina M. Coy*
El Cajon, California
23 21

• • • • • • • •

BE RESPONSIVE TO ODD REQUESTS. When my wife was eight months pregnant, we got in a cab at two in the morning because she needed cheese on a bagel from her favorite diner.

—*Bill*
Boston, Massachusetts
- 2

• • • • • • • •

ASK WHAT SHE NEEDS. Never assume that you know, and never under any circumstances attempt to tell her what she needs.

—*Pat Q.T.*
Oakland, California
32 27

• • • • • • • •

LISTEN TO YOUR WIFE'S COMPLAINTS and validate her feelings as much as possible. Pregnancy and early motherhood are especially difficult times for a woman.

—*Beth*
Oklahoma
6

GET WHATEVER YOUR WIFE WANTS WHEN SHE'S PREGNANT, whenever she wants it. And be grateful that now there are 7-11s and 24-hour grocery stores.

—*ANONYMOUS*
REDMOND, WASHINGTON
5 3

HELP OUT MORE WITH THE household chores when your wife is pregnant. Some guys don't think they need to do this, but frankly, they're the ones who end up divorced.

—*MARK CRANE*
AURORA, COLORADO
12 9

RUB YOUR PREGNANT WIFE'S FEET whenever she asks.

—*LYNN JONES*
KIRKLAND, WASHINGTON
8 5

MY HUSBAND AND I TOOK A ONE-DAY (condensed) birthing class, which was extremely effective. We learned breathing techniques, so that I'd understand what my body was going through during delivery.

—*JENNIFER SEILER*
SAN RAFAEL, CALIFORNIA

Embrace cravings but make sure you don't go overboard. Balanced eating habits are best.

—*ANONYMOUS*
AUSTIN, TEXAS
6

• • • • • • • •

I PERSONALLY FOUND THE WHOLE PROCESS really enjoyable—I didn't have morning sickness, I thought it was cool watching my body change, and my labor only lasted about five hours. Like anything else in life, getting pregnant is what you make of it.

—*WENDI K.*
PARKER, COLORADO
8 5

• • • • • • • •

> "Before we had children, my husband and I built a home office, did tons of spring-cleaning, prepared the baby's room and tried to see as many movies as possible."

—*T.N.*
HUNTINGTON BEACH, CALIFORNIA
19M 3.5M

• • • • • • • •

CHILDBIRTH IS DIRECTLY CORRELATED to the full moon and falling barometric pressure, so plan on the baby coming around the full moon of the due date, or during a hurricane.

—*SHELLEY*
TAMPA, FLORIDA
17 12

MOMMY'S HAVING A BABY...

PREPARE YOUR CHILD WHEN A NEW BABY IS COMING! I talked about the new baby that was on the way with both my children. Once my daughter had arrived, I let her brother and sister hold and care for her so they didn't feel left out. It's easy for children to become jealous of a new baby if they are excluded from the process.

—*BEATRICE*
MIAMI, FLORIDA
5 2 8M

• • • • • • • •

DON'T GET DISCOURAGED WHEN your new baby's older brother says, "I don't want a baby brother, I want a pet pig!" or, "Can you take him back to Sears now?"

—*JUDY C.*
SPRINGFIELD, ILLINOIS
33 28 25 21

• • • • • • • •

WHEN I WAS EXPECTING MY SECOND CHILD, I prepared my daughter for the changes to come. My husband and I told her that our neighbor from next door was going to come over and take care of her while Mommy and Daddy were at the hospital. So my daughter was expecting to be taken care of, and she knew that a baby was on the way home.

—*DEE RUSSELL*
HONEDYE FALLS, NEW YORK
24 22 14

• • • • • • • •

I WAS NERVOUS ABOUT TELLING MY SON about my pregnancy. I sat him on the couch and talked to him about his friends with baby brothers and sisters. I showed him my tummy and told him a baby was growing in there. When my husband came home, he said, "Guess what? Mom's going to have a baby!"

—*A.T.*
ARLINGTON, MASSACHUSETTS
4 3M

AS SOON AS YOU FIND OUT YOU'RE PREGNANT I suggest you do the following: go out to dinner, the movies and all the other things you like to do as much as possible; go on a nice, relaxing vacation; try to get everything you need before the baby arrives, because it's hard to get the essentials after the fact. Finally, have an honest discussion with your spouse about your fears, expectations and love for one another, because the world is about to change!

—VANESSA WILKINSON
COLORA, MARYLAND
5 3

INFANT INFO

For couples trying to conceive, 20 percent will become pregnant in the first month, 50 percent will be pregnant by six months, and 85 percent will be pregnant by the end of one year.

ONE OF THE BENEFITS OF BEING PREGNANT IS THAT YOUR BOOBS get a lot bigger. But then again, so does your butt.

—ANONYMOUS
NEW YORK, NEW YORK

THE BIGGEST PROBLEM FOR ME during my pregnancy was getting a good night's sleep—I just couldn't train myself to sleep on my side. I'd often be awake at 3:30 a.m., with no hope of falling back asleep. The up side is that I trained myself to "get by" on five hours of sleep per night, so dealing with my infant and her sleep schedule didn't take a lot of adjustment on my part.

—A.
BERKELEY, CALIFORNIA
2

MY WIFE SUGGESTED WE FORGET LAMAZE CLASS. She said, "This baby is coming out whether I breathe correctly or not. Let's not waste our time."

—MARC A. CLAYBON
GOLDEN, COLORADO
15M

2 Birth: A Very Special Delivery

You might not have believed it a month ago, but it's true what they say—that baby's coming out of you. Whether you go into labor in the middle of the night and scramble for the hospital, or you wake up early and scramble to make your scheduled C-section, having a baby is the experience of a lifetime. And it's different for everyone. Here's a primer.

ONE OF THE HARDEST PARTS ABOUT HAVING A BABY is actually having the baby. Make sure to scream loudly in jubilation and celebration!

—*LOIS*
BURIEN, WASHINGTON

LABOR'S NOT AS TOUGH AS EVERYONE TELLS YOU. IT WAS THE GREATEST DAY OF MY LIFE.

—*M.H.*
13M

MAKE SURE YOU LEAVE EXTRA ROOM for rush hour. There was just nothing more frustrating in the world than being stuck in slow traffic for the birth of our son. Luckily, we still made it to the hospital, but we cut it much closer than we would have liked.

—*DEKE*
SAN DIEGO, CALIFORNIA
13 10

• • • • • • • •

MY WATER BROKE A MONTH EARLY with our second child. My husband, John, was at the other end of the house in our room. We didn't have anything ready for the hospital. I wandered around the house in a fog putting my bag together, while my husband followed behind me saying, "You don't need that. We have to GO!"

—*PAT CURRY*
WATKINSVILLE, GEORGIA
17 15

When it comes to childbirth, no matter how much you prepare, you can't know what it will be like until you're in the middle of it. Just be ready for whatever may come.

—*JEANNIE SPONHEIM*
LOVELAND, COLORADO

• • • • • • • •

I HAD PLANNED FROM THE BEGINNING to have a home birth. I was at peace with the idea up until an hour before my daughter was born. At that point I was screaming to be taken to the hospital! But my friend, a midwife, was there, and she reminded me that I wanted a home birth, and to stay true to that. With no regrets, I got what I wanted.

—*JEANNE-MARIE CROWE*
FAIRFAX, CALIFORNIA
11W

MAKE SURE THAT WHATEVER YOU EAT during labor is yummy (jello, juice, banana) because that's what you're going to taste if you throw up, which I did repeatedly with both kids. Not pretty advice, but I pass it on (unsolicited, of course) to all my pregnant friends.

—*D.K.*
FOSTER CITY, CALIFORNIA
3 1

"When my wife was in labor with our daughter the doctor said, 'Do you want an epidural?' And I said, 'Yes, *I'll* take one.'"

—*EDDIE FINKELSTEIN*
CHAPPAQUA, NEW YORK
16 14 9

MY DAUGHTER WAS BORN NINE WEEKS EARLY and I was completely ill-prepared because there were no signs indicating I would have a pre-term baby. In fact, I had ignored the chapters in my baby books that dealt with premature babies. You think it won't happen to you, so you skip those sections. Don't!

—*SUZANNE WILLIN*
WOODACRE, CALIFORNIA
2

I always said I didn't care if my baby was a boy or girl, but the second I heard "girl" I was so sure that's what I'd always wanted!

—*FRANK*
RENO, NEVADA
1

TIMING IS EVERYTHING

My wife's contractions began around midnight. At two in the morning we called our midwife for guidance and she told us to wait until the contractions were one to two minutes apart. We timed the contractions with a stopwatch all night, but it wasn't consistent. They would get close together, then spread out again. At eight o'clock we called the doctor's office, and the nurse said the same thing—contractions should be one to two minutes apart. By eleven a.m. my wife had been in labor for nearly 12 hours, so we decided to go to the hospital. I was loading the car when my wife waddled out. She tried to get in the car, and physically could not do it. She realized the baby was coming right then and there. She stood up, lowered her pants, and gave birth to our child in the driveway! One push and he came right out. I ran around the side of the car and the first words my child heard were "Holy shit!" A neighbor called 911, and the paramedics and an ambulance arrived and mother and baby were whisked off to the hospital.

—*Brian*
Ft. Myers, Florida
4 1

• • • • • • • •

Make sure your car works! When my wife went into labor, we had a one-hour drive to the hospital. Along the way, I kept noticing my car lights getting dimmer and dimmer until finally, the alternator went out and the car died. At two a.m. I had my pregnant wife in the driver's seat while I pushed our car uphill to the Denny's parking lot so I could call my mom to pick us up. We nearly named our first child Denny because of that experience.

—*John Cooke*
Greeley, Colorado
23 21

WE WENT FLYING OVER THE BRIDGE TO PORTLAND with me screaming over every bump. When we got to the hospital the first thing I said was "Oh my God, give me a shot, I can't handle the pain." The doctor examined me and looked at the nurse and said, "Fully!" Meaning fully dilated, move it! I had my daughter an hour later.

—*Sarah Goldberg*
South Portland, Maine
16 8

• • • • • • • •

WE WERE TRAVELING ACROSS COUNTRY FROM VERMONT to California when I went into labor in Utah—two months early. And to make matters worse, we were driving along I-70 where there are signs lining the highway that say "no services," "no rest stops," "no exits." I delivered him at a truck stop along the interstate. Under "place of birth," my son's birth certificate says "Mile Marker 140, I-70E!"

—*C.C.*
San Francisco, California
1

• • • • • • • •

I WENT INTO LABOR AROUND 10:00 P.M.. The doctor thought I had plenty of time, but I was in serious labor within 15 minutes. We jumped in the car but it was out of gas! We had to stop at a gas station on the way, and I knew the baby was coming right there. We barely made it to the hospital. To this day, I don't know if my doctor made it or if someone else delivered my son!

—*Nola Smith*
Tampa, Florida
41 35

READY OR NOT!

The day I woke up in labor I was in complete denial about it. Instead of calling my doctor, I decided to go to the movies. My husband kept asking, "Shouldn't you go to the hospital?" But I just waved goodbye and told him I'd call when the time came. Halfway through the movie my contractions got so bad that I left the theater and drove to the doctor's office. I was six centimeters dilated. The doctor told me to call my husband so he could pick me up and drive me to the hospital. I ignored him and instead called my husband and told him to meet me at the hospital. As I drove myself there, I remember thinking "What a beautiful day." The sky was bright. The sun was sparkling off the snow. I got to the hospital still not thinking that I was really about to give birth. I was prepared to walk the halls and wait for my husband to arrive. But, as soon as the nurse saw me she said "Lie down!" I had my daughter a few minutes later.

—Deb
Orono, Maine
18

MY WIFE HAD TWO EMERGENCY C-SECTIONS. It was so stressful because I had to choose between following the baby or staying with my wife while they finished the surgery. I chose the baby both times because that's what my wife wanted, but I really wish that we'd had a friend or family member with us to stay with her.

—*JERRY B.*
NEW YORK, NEW YORK
3 1

"I think the first time the reality that I was going to be a father hit me was when my wife's water broke. That was when the whole thing sank in."

—*TIM*
SOUTH PORTLAND, MAINE
7

DO NOT LET YOUR BIRTH COACH OUT OF YOUR SIGHT for more than a minute when you're in labor. My husband stepped out to get food and I completely panicked. When he came back, I'd turned into Linda Blair in "The Exorcist."

—*DIANA LAWTON*
WESTFORD, MASSACHUSETTS
2

Childbirth is one of the few chances there are in life to see a miracle.

—*WAYNE DRASH*
ATLANTA, GEORGIA
2

I WAS NERVOUS ABOUT HAVING AN EPIDURAL because people said it slowed labor down, but I really couldn't handle the pain so I did it anyway. The epidural ended up relaxing me so much that it kicked my labor into high gear. I went from four centimeters dilated to ready to push in about an hour.

—*MELODY WARNICK*
ST. GEORGE, UTAH
2

"Drugs are a good thing. When you break your leg, or go to the dentist, they don't say, 'Breathe through the pain.'"

—*MARET VAN FLEET*
ELLICOT CITY, MARYLAND
8 6

There's no way you can plan a birth. The process is just too unpredictable.

—*KARA JOHNSTON*
KLAMATH FALLS, OREGON
5 13M

I HAD A SPINAL EPIDURAL and couldn't feel my legs for about twelve hours afterwards. I hated that, so I never did it again. I opted for natural childbirth for the next three.

—*LORI T.*
CHARLESTON, SOUTH CAROLINA
36 34 31 26

A MAN'S PLACE

JUST MAKE SURE YOU'RE THERE. That's the best advice a man can get about surviving the birth of his baby.

—DAVE CASPERSON
WICHITA, KANSAS
40 37 34

• • • • • • • •

YOUR ROLE IN THE DELIVERY ROOM is to get ice chips and rub her back (at least, until the epidural is in). And whatever you do, please don't take anything said by the mother-to-be during labor personally.

—KEITH REGAN
GRAFTON, MASSACHUSETTS
5 3

• • • • • • • •

THE BEST THING THAT DADS CAN DO is to just be there, standing, legs slightly bent, ready to run out the door for your wife's every request, as fast as you can. And yes, you must remain in this stance for however long it takes. (I recommend a regimen of squat-thrusts for a few weeks beforehand.) It's almost like the mother-to-be is at a virtual computer, and the dad-to-be is the cursor, and she moves you around the screen. She might click you on the Need A Glass Of Water icon, or the Grab Somebody, I Need Something For The Pain icon.

—DAVID E. LISS
PENNINGTON, NEW JERSEY
4 1

• • • • • • • •

DIRECT ALL YOUR ATTENTION TO YOUR WIFE in the delivery room. Breathe deep and look at her reassuringly in the eyes—no matter how much you want to pass out at the sight of all that blood.

—RUSS COX
PORTLAND MAINE
-5 1

GIVING BIRTH AT HOME WAS WONDERFUL. I was able to stay in my own bed and to sleep as much as I was wanted after the birth—which was not much, because I kept staring at my new baby in utter astonishment.

—*NANCY ENGLISH*
PORTLAND, MAINE

• • • • • • • •

WHEN I WAS IN LABOR, A NURSE SUGGESTED that doing squats might help me ease the pain during contractions. So when the next one hit, I started doing squats, and counted how many I could do in a contraction—10. The nurse said the contractions would get harder, but not longer. So for the rest of my labor, I knew that when a contraction hit, it would be over in 10 squats. Focusing on counting the squats instead of focusing on the pain helped me get through it. Once I had to be in bed for the delivery, I simply counted my breaths instead. That was the strategy I needed. It eased my labor, and I got through the pain—10 squats at a time!

—*ROBYN*
BIGLERVILLE, PENNSYLVANIA
1

If you live near a major league ballpark, make sure you have a copy of the home game schedule so you'll know if ballgame traffic will pose a problem or not.

—*LISBETH LEVINE*
CHICAGO, ILLINOIS
6 4

• • • • • • • •

MY MOTHER WAS A HUGE PAIN IN THE BUTT during labor—constantly asking the nurse what everything was, and she was a nervous wreck, which just made me nervous. Finally, when the time came, I was excited to be able to kick her out of the delivery room!

—*ADRIANE*
FT. LAUDERDALE, FLORIDA
1

MY WIFE FOUND THAT IT HELPED HER A LOT if I pushed hard on her hips as she was having the contractions. My arms hurt after a while from all the isometric exercise, but I couldn't very well complain about the pain, now could I!

—*FRANK*
RENO, NEVADA
1

"Dads, ask the doctor if you can cut the cord when your baby is born. It will make you feel more connected with this tiny new baby."

—*M.F.*
SAN FRANCISCO, CALIFORNIA
1M

OUR YOUNGER DAUGHTER WAS BORN PREMATURELY. I left the hospital after 24 hours, but she had to stay for 30 days. It's so horrible to leave the hospital without your baby. Hospital visits were difficult because my older daughter was two at the time, and two-year-olds don't fit in well at the NICU. To make it work, we asked friends and family to come with us to the hospital and sit with our daughter in the waiting room while we visited our baby.

—*KRISTEN*
BETHLEHEM, PENNSYLVANIA
3 18M

For me labor was fantastic. I didn't have to do anything. (I had a surrogate mother.)

—*CATHY RAFF*
MACCABIM, ISRAEL
8 5 3

HINDSIGHT

We were stationed in Gabon (Africa) when I got pregnant with our first child. We thought about going to Paris (where my husband is from), or the U.S., but I figured women here have babies every day; why should I be any different? So I decided I'd have the baby there. My doctor assured me that they had the necessary equipment should there be any emergency. I had to buy all my own medical supplies—the epidural, saline solution, rubber gloves, etc.

Although our son had a little trouble breathing at first, everything went fine with the birth. But I didn't find out until later, that if there had been a medical emergency, I would have had to fly to France to get to the best facility. It was a frightening realization. I hadn't checked out the clinic enough, and they misrepresented their emergency services. Now I often think of that phrase, "God protects children and fools." I fall into the "fool" category for blissfully, blindly thinking everything should go fine. I would never make a decision like that again.

—A.O.
MARIETTA, GEORGIA
4 2

CONSIDER GETTING A DOULA to accompany you for the delivery. She is experienced in childbirth, will stick up for your rights as a patient, and can help keep you calm.

—*LISA COHEN*
BROOKLYN, NEW YORK
7W

I BROUGHT IN PICTURES OF MY NIECE, who I am completely ga-ga about, to look at while I was in labor. When the pain was at its worst, the pictures really helped me focus, and reminded me that it would all be worth it in the end.

—*CEECEE*
RENO, NEVADA
1

MY FIRST BABY HAD TO BE SUCTIONED OUT. My second required forceps. The third time around, I was lucky to be paired up with an exceptional nurse, who not only explained every step of the process in great detail, but she told me specifically which muscles to use when I pushed. This made the delivery so much easier and faster. I was like, "Oh, so *that's* how you're supposed to do it!" I can't believe it took me three babies to figure out the correct muscles to use.

—*STEPHANIE ISMERT*
CENTENNIAL, COLORADO
8 6 1

DADS, BE YOUR WIFE'S ADVOCATE IN THE HOSPITAL. Fight for privacy, quiet, whatever she needs, even if it means you have to play the heavy with medical staff and even inquiring relatives.

—*DAN DUPONT*
ARLINGTON, VIRGINIA
6 3 3M

When my doctor asked what kind of childbirth experience I wanted, I told him the same as my mom—they knocked her out and woke her up when it was over.

—*MARET VAN FLEET*
ELLICOT CITY, MARYLAND
8 6

DREAM COME TRUE

When I was pregnant with my fourth, I already had three sons. Whenever we would go anywhere as a family, total strangers would say, "I hope you get a girl this time." I always responded by spouting the usual, "Oh, it doesn't matter to me as long as it's healthy," but I secretly agreed, hoping it would be a girl.

My husband was convinced it would be yet another boy. Whenever I would linger over the pink sleepers and pink dresses and ruffled panties, he would remind me how silly those would look on a boy. As I approached full term, the doctor estimated that the baby could be 10 or 11 pounds—seeming to indicate that it would indeed be a boy.

I was scheduled for a C-section. During the birth I heard the doctor saying, "My gosh, she looks like a three-month-old!" as he lifted our daughter up above the sheet for me and my husband to see. I started crying and said, "I got my little girl!" And Jay held me close and corrected me, "*We* got our little girl."

—*Elizabeth J.*
Lansing, Michigan
13 11 8 20M

OUR DAUGHTER WAS BORN during the 1997 Super Bowl. The home team—the New England Patriots—were in the game so I was less than useful in the delivery room. Doctors came in and out of the room throughout the labor, talking about the game but never saying who was ahead. I would ask, plaintively, from my position in the "cheap seats," who was winning, but no one even acknowledged the question.

—*TIM*
SOUTH PORTLAND, MAINE
7

IN THE HOSPITAL, AFTER HAVING SEVERAL VISITS from family and friends and hospital staff, my husband turned the phone off and set up camp outside of my room. He sat there while I slept for an hour and a half (which seemed like heaven at the time) and would not let anyone in to see me, even the nurses. Needless to say he got away with it for about 90 minutes before they insisted on coming in my room.

—*ANGELA STAHL*
MILWAUKEE, WISCONSIN
3.5M

WE DIDN'T TURN ON OUR VIDEO CAMERA until after the delivery because I wanted to be a part of the birth, and not a photographer. Instead we got awesome footage of my daughter getting cleaned up, being weighed and measured, and her mother holding her for the first time. They're great shots because my wife was no longer in pain. She was just happy.

—*STEVE MACY*
PARKER, COLORADO
2

FIVE SIGNS OF LABOR

1. Bloody show (a pink stain on your underwear or toilet tissue)
2. Your water breaks
3. Regular contractions that intensify
4. Pain in lower back
5. Cramps that feel like intestinal upset

HINT TO HUSBANDS WHOSE WIVES ARE IN LABOR: Don't stand around talking to the nurses about sports while your wife has contractions.

—CATHY K.
KIRKLAND, WASHINGTON

MY HUSBAND HAD THE GALL TO COMPLAIN that he didn't have time to finish the Coke that the nurses had given him in the delivery room because the labor happened so fast.

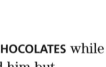

—GRETCHEN ROBERTS
PALO ALTO, CALIFORNIA
1

MY HUSBAND PASSED AROUND CHOCOLATES while I was in labor. The nurses loved him but completely ignored me!

—LESLIE
MERRICK, NEW YORK
-5

BE CAREFUL IN THE HOSPITAL. They tried to give me the wrong baby—twice! The nurse kept getting confused, and I had to tell her she had the wrong kid. Believe me, though, many times I wish I had kept my mouth shut.

—ADAIR MORELAND
KEARNY, NEW JERSEY

3 The Name Game: How to Choose?

You think pregnancy is overwhelming? Now you've actually got to decide what to call this child—for the rest of his or her life! Before you've even met! When it comes to naming your baby, you want to get it right, or you'll have a lot of explaining to do—to your child, your in-laws, your friends, your child's friends . . . But fear not. There is a method to the name-game madness. Plenty of them, in fact.

ASK YOURSELF IF ANY OF FOLLOWING sentences sound silly:
1. "Can <kid's name> come out to play?"
2. "I love you, <kid's name>."
3. "Let's make <kid's name> the head of the company."

—*MARRIT INGMAN*
AUSTIN, TEXAS
2

IF YOU HAVE AN UNUSUAL LAST NAME, PICK A SIMPLE FIRST NAME FOR YOUR BABY.

—*ANONYMOUS*
PARIS, MISSOURI
10 8

I PICKED A NAME BASED ON A COMIC CHARACTER, added my mother's middle name and presented it to my husband. He liked it and that was it—quick and easy choice. We did, however, double-check initials and spellings for "teasing factors." We were both picked on in school and I wanted to minimize it as much as possible for my daughter.

—*STACI PRIEST*
PFLUGERVILLE, TEXAS
20M

We had four books of names. From them we each made a list of the names we liked. The strange thing is we only looked at girl names, even before we knew we were having a girl.

—*ALLAN JAFFE*
PETALUMA, CALIFORNIA
21 6

WE KEPT CHANGING OUR MIND about the baby's name, and each time we did, our family said, "Oh, we like that name so much better than the last one." When everyone finally said, "Oh, we like the new name but we also like old one" we knew we had a winner.

—*JONATHAN & JULIANA ROLLINS*
MARIETTA, GEORGIA
11W

HOW DO PEOPLE HAVE THE NAMES PICKED out before the baby is born? It seems like such an emotional process. We didn't want to know if we were having a boy or a girl, which added to the excitement, but it also meant we couldn't settle on a name until the baby had arrived.

—*SUZANNE WILLIN*
WOODACRE, CALIFORNIA
2

I KEPT A BOWL AT MY DESK AT WORK, and people wrote down names and dropped them in the bowl. At the end of each week I'd go through them. I made my selection from my co-workers' suggestions.

—*P.W.*
CHICAGO, ILLINOIS
9

MY WIFE WANTED A JEWISH NAME, and I wanted one that was easy to spell, easy to pronounce, and not overly common. We went through a book of baby names and each came up with a short list of names we liked. Of course there was no intersection between our lists. It took months for us to finally agree.

—DAVID HUBBELL
KIRKLAND, WASHINGTON
6

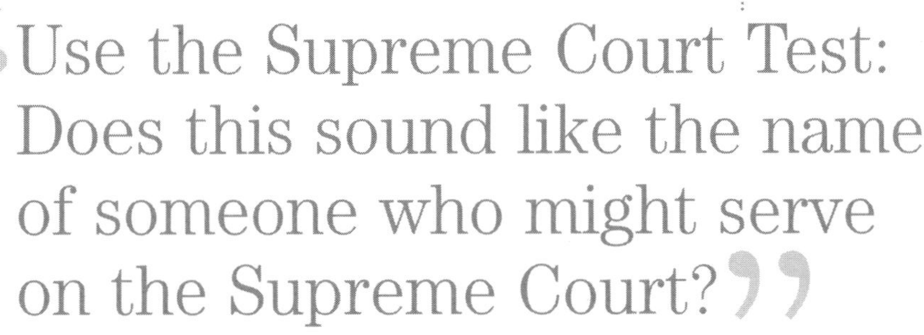
“Use the Supreme Court Test: Does this sound like the name of someone who might serve on the Supreme Court?”

—LINDA ANDREWS REEVES
SAN ANTONIO, TEXAS
10 5

Don't pick names with initials that spell some-thing weird.

—MARK SCOTT
SAFFORD, ARIZONA
16 13

MY HUBBY HAD A HARD TIME DECIDING on a name, so we started calling baby Tommy (after his father), until we could decide. By the time my son was born, I had called him Tommy for so long that changing it was out of the question.

—HEIDE A.W. KAMINSKI
TECUMSEH, MICHIGAN
18 15 6

BEWARE OF SHARING

Don't tell people the baby name you've picked out when you're still pregnant unless you want feedback. You will get feedback; believe me! And even though you think people will be polite and tactful, they won't. I shared the name ideas I had for my first son and ended up changing it at least three or four times. I kept getting responses like, "Oh, that name doesn't sound good with your last name." Or, "Oh, I dated a boy with that name just before I met your father, and your dad was always so jealous." And, "He'll have to spell that all the time." It was so frustrating that my husband and I finally decided to pick a name and keep our mouths shut. Sure enough, once the baby was born, nobody had the heart, or nerve, to criticize the name we chose.

—*Heidi*
Chicago, Illinois
14 11 6

In the Hispanic tradition, the father names his first son after himself, but I didn't want to do that. Instead, we went with names we liked—Jacqueline and Nicholas. Though we did give one nod to tradition by giving my son the middle name Francisco—after my grandfather.

—*Rick Barbero*
Gaithersburg, Maryland
12 5

WHEN MY HUSBAND AND I REALIZED what Pam Irene Garber's or David Oliver Garber's monograms would be, we reconsidered our selections.

—Rose
Los Angeles, California
2

• • • • • • • • •

“When you watch your wife go through all the pain of labor to deliver your beautiful baby, you will realize that she deserves to choose the baby's name.”

—M.F.
San Francisco, California
1M

INFANT INFO

Emily has been the most popular girl's name since 1996.

• • • • • • • • •

I WANTED TO NAME MY KIDS “Penelope,” “Peter,” “Patricia” and “Petula.” Our last name is “Papas.” I thought it was cute. But my husband said, “Don't you dare!” We ended up with family names: “Christy,” “James,” “Mia” and “Nikole.”

—Mary Jane Papas
Brooklyn, New York
36 34 32 29

Don't share your proposed baby names with other people when you're pregnant. I've had names stolen.

—*MARYBETH*
SAN FRANCISCO, CALIFORNIA
4

RESIST THE IMPULSE TO GIVE YOUR KIDS names that match, like "Mike, Mark, and Michelle." It may seem cute when they're babies, but believe me—I speak from experience here—when they get a little older, they will resent the hell out of you!

—*MISSY*
DETROIT, MICHIGAN
14 12 9

IT'S ALWAYS GOOD TO ONE-UP YOUR FAMILY when you name your kid. My wife's mother lost out to her brother when selecting a name, because his baby was born first. There was no competition when we had our first child, so we got to use the name we wanted.

—*JIM FALKENSTEIN*
NORTH HOLLYWOOD, CALIFORNIA
8 5

A RATIONAL APPROACH

We each sat down with a stack of name books and a piece of paper. On one side we wrote our choices for first names, and on the other side we wrote choices for middle names. Then, we traded lists. We each scratched off any name we could not live with. Then, we got our original lists back, and numbered the names in order of favorite to least favorite. It turned out we both had the same first name on our top five so that's what we used. Then we flipped the papers over to see which middle names best matched the one we had selected. I advise all parents to use this method. It worked, and it was pain-free.

—*JESSICA L. DELANEY*
JOHNSTOWN, COLORADO
4 2

AS LONG AS THE MOTHER AND FATHER of the baby like the name, that's all that really matters! I've heard of parents keeping the name that they have chosen secret until the baby's arrival to avoid any negative input from outsiders.

—EMBER NEVILL
FORT WORTH, TEXAS
20M

THERE WERE NO ARGUMENTS OR DISCUSSIONS; naming our babies was easy. All three of my children are named after their grandparents.

—ANONYNOUS
CHICAGO, ILLINOIS
19 17 15

INFANT INFO

Jacob has been the most popular boy's name since 1999.

I COULDN'T DECIDE ON A NAME for my oldest daughter for almost a week after she was born.

—SUE WILLIAMS-JUDGE
SEATTLE, WASHINGTON
12 9

AFTER THIRTEEN HOURS OF LABOR, I held our newborn son in my arms and sweetly said to my husband that I really wanted a certain name. He simply couldn't refuse.

—LORAINE BRANCATTO BOERSMA
TOLEDO, OHIO
6 4

WE AGREED THAT IF THE BABY WAS A GIRL, my spouse would get to name her, and if it was a boy, I'd get to name him. Both of us retained full veto powers, however.

—JOHN RODGERS
SEATTLE, WASHINGTON
9

We asked all of our friends the names of their children's classmates and friends. It gave us lots of good ideas.

—*Christine B.*
New York, New York
4M

If you want to name a baby after a special person in your life, but you don't like his or her name, just use it as the middle name.

—*N. Clark*
Houston, Texas
15

We were going to call our first son Matthew Alexander, which would have given him the initials M.A.D! We just could not do that to him—even if it does fit our family perfectly!

—*Lynda DiFrancesco*
Raleigh, North Carolina
2 2M

Be sure to do an online search for the meaning of any names you like. It turns out my son's name means "Little Fire." He certainly lives up to it; he is a little fire!

—*Erin Callahan*
Kershaw, South Carolina
2

4

Coming Home: The Fourth Trimester

Call it Mother Nature's Boot Camp. The first three months of a baby's life are among the hardest for new parents—and it starts when you walk out of the hospital and make your way home. No matter how much you think you've prepared, you're still learning as you go. What do you need? How do you handle all the new responsibilities? How do you survive? Ten-hut! Read on.

BEFORE HAVING CHILDREN, I HAD NEVER considered myself a maternal person. But then one day you're holding your newborn baby in your arms and it sets in: "Wow, I was made to do this."

—*O.C.*
SAN FRANCISCO, CALIFORNIA
5 2

THERE'S NOTHING MORE REWARDING THAN A LITTLE CRITTER MADE WITH HALF YOUR GERMS.

—*DICKIE*
ATLANTA, GEORGIA
6M

When my daughter first came home from the hospital, it struck me that there were no nurses or doctors to help us care for our baby. At first, this thought instilled panic in me. But then we just did it.

—*Sean Keller*
East Moline, Illinois
2

You really don't need someone else staying with you. If you need someone else to stay, I don't think you've grown up enough to handle a baby.

—*Anonymous*
Mason, Michigan
48 46 45
44 42 40

When my wife and I prepared for our baby's first bath, it took both of us to do it—one to hold the camera and the instruction book, and the other to actually bathe the baby.

—*Kevin Sholander*
Fort Collins, Colorado
12 10

No one gives you operating instructions on taking this baby home. I spent so much time preparing for the birth, then, all of a sudden they said, "OK, you can take her home." I could've stayed there a month.

—*Cynthia*
Portland, Maine
2

Make sure the child seat is in the car before the kid is born. My son was a month early and my father-in-law and I had to install the seat in the dark. After we took the baby home, we took the car to the state trooper who inspects baby seats. He just shook his head and said, "You would have been safer just holding him on your lap."

—*Tom Harris*
Waynesboro, Virginia
3 1

TAKE CARE OF YOURSELF PHYSICALLY and mentally during this period and don't neglect your needs. Rely on your spouse to do as much as possible. Get on a good health routine as soon as possible. I did, and it worked wonders.

—*DAWN RODRIGUEZ*
PASSAIC, NEW JERSEY

"Mom and Dad should take a break at the same time so that the two of you can spend time together without the baby."

—*ANONYMOUS*
ALAMEDA, CALIFORNIA
7M

WHEN WE BROUGHT OUR SON HOME from the hospital, the most overwhelming thing for us was the sheets and sheets of paper instructing us on how to care for him, feed him, keep him happy and safe. After a couple of months together, we found out that our son teaches us what he needs. When we threw away the pieces of paper and focused on him, it went so much better.

—*DAN STUHLFATZ*
CONWAY SPRINGS, KANSAS
3

Mom is busy taking care of the baby, Dad is busy taking care of Mom.

—*D. EVANS*
OREGON CITY, OREGON
8 5

LOVE AT 122ND SIGHT

Do not expect to love your baby wholeheartedly right away. Love at first sight doesn't work with adults, so there's no reason to think it'll work with a newborn. You acquire this blob which doesn't do anything other than cry, eat and poop, and in return you get sleep deprivation, lack of a social life, no sex, and your spouse becoming a whole lot less fun (not that I was a barrel of laughs, either). Honestly, the best part of the day was going to work, where I could look forward to nine to ten hours in a baby-free zone. It probably wasn't until my daughter was four months that I was completely won over by her charm and smile. That's when I really "got into" being a dad.

—*Mark Kaplan*
Foster City, California
3 1

One big thing that changes in your life is that you lose spontaneity. But we have wonderful (child-less) friends who come over to our house, to have a great meal and hang out at home. We prefer this to going out because babysitters are $12/hour, so a night out means paying twice—for dinner with your husband and then another $40 to the babysitter.

—*Melissa Stein*
3

The night I brought my new son home from the hospital my older son said, "We are not as happy as we used to be." When the nurse left, he ran after her crying, "You forgot to take the baby!"

—*Anonymous*
Baltimore, Maryland
34 31

SEEK OUT ADVICE FROM PEOPLE YOU RESPECT. In this age of information overload, it's easy to get confused and fearful trying to sort out all the different theories on the right and wrong way to raise children.

—*CHERYL PERLITZ*
GLENVIEW, ILLINOIS
36 33 31

"Babies are like bowling balls. Unless you're trying, they're a lot harder to break than you think."

—*JONATHAN & JULIANA ROLLINS*
MARIETTA, GEORGIA
11W

I LIKEN THE FIRST THREE MONTHS after childbirth as the "fourth trimester." You get no sleep, you can't predict your schedule, running errands becomes difficult, you can't just pop into the dry cleaners, you have to take the baby everywhere you go. But remember, there is a light at the end of the tunnel.

—*T.N.*
HUNTINGTON BEACH, CALIFORNIA
19M 3.5M

MAKE SURE YOU HAVE A HELPER AROUND, whether it's a friend, nanny, mother-in-law or a doula—anyone who will offer you unconditional support and will not criticize your choices or methods.

—*D. EVANS*
OREGON CITY, OREGON
8 5

One of the everyday benefits of having a baby is you meet lots of new parents. It is a whole new world.

—*SKYE FERRANTE*
NEW YORK,
NEW YORK

LITTLE HELPERS

INCLUDE OLDER CHILDREN IN THE CARE OF THE BABY. Ask them to help fold clothes. Set an alarm clock and ask them to remind you when it goes off so you know it's time to feed the baby. Compliment them on helping mommy.

—JANET VALLONE
WAYMART, PENNSYLVANIA
34 31 27

• • • • • • • •

MY SON WAS FIVE WHEN HIS SISTER WAS BORN. I remember him watching me bathe and dress the baby when I brought her home. He said, "Babies are hard trouble, aren't they?" I got him involved by asking him to be a runner for things I needed. It helped him feel like a big brother.

—ANONYMOUS
RAYMORE, MISSOURI

• • • • • • • •

WATCH THAT BABY CLOSELY WITH OLDER SIBLINGS. My daughter thought the baby was her baby. He was just a few weeks old when I caught her holding him around the middle, carrying him down the hall. She was way too little to do that—and the baby seemed ill-at-ease for the rest of the day.

—DOLORES JOHNSON
WICHITA, KANSAS
50 48 45

• • • • • • • •

GIVE THE OLDER SIBLINGS RESPONSIBILITIES WITH THE BABY to keep them from getting jealous. My older kids absolutely love helping feed her, hold her, and play with her. Helping their baby sister makes them feel important.

—TABITHA MOTT
CHEYENNE, WYOMING
10 7 5.5M

I MADE SURE TO CREATE A SENSE OF FAIRNESS BETWEEN MY CHILDREN. If I played with my two-year-old, I'd explain, "OK, I've got to take care of the baby now." When I was done with the baby and needed to get back to my older child, I'd tell the baby (in front of my older child, of course), "OK, I've got to take care of your brother now." It created a sense of balance and fairness for my older child.

—KIRSTEN
FORT COLLINS, COLORADO
6 3

• • • • • • • •

TIME REALLY IS THE ONLY WAY FOR A CONNECTION to build between a big sibling and a new baby. At first my older son would push the baby away and say, "No." But now, they just love hanging out together and they're inseparable. In the first two years, though, he liked his bunny a lot more.

—ERIC FALKENSTEIN
EDEN PRAIRIE, MINNESOTA
5 3

FEED THE PARENTS

SEND MEALS TO THE NEW PARENTS' HOME. Mom and Dad won't have time to cook. It's a caring, thoughtful gesture. Parents need that more than they need one more copy of "Goodnight Moon."

—*T.P.*
LARKSPUR, CALIFORNIA
4

• • • • • • • •

IF ANYONE ASKS WHAT YOU NEED, tell them to bring dinner! New parents have no ability to feed themselves and take care of a newborn. We would have starved to death without the generosity of our friends and family.

—*ELIZABETH LEFFERT HEISE*
CORAL GABLES, FLORIDA
3M

• • • • • • • •

ONE OF THE BEST GIFTS WE RECEIVED after our first child was born was a gift certificate for a dinner out and a promise of babysitting for the evening.

—*KAREN SATHER*
DALLAS, TEXAS
7 6

53

WE WERE TOTALLY OVERWHELMED by having twins. We were first-time parents and we were both learning how to care for two babies and learning how to create a family with twice the need, all in a sleepless stupor. If it were not for our friends, family, church and community who came and quietly fed us, wiped babies' bottoms, and generally looked after the zombie parents, our new little family would not have gotten the wonderful start it did. It didn't take a village; it took a city.

—*RUSS COX*
PORTLAND, MAINE
-5 1

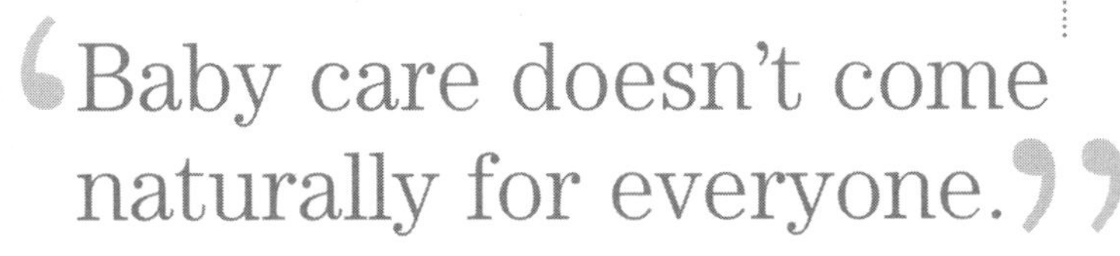
“Baby care doesn't come naturally for everyone.”

—*KEVIN SHOLANDER*
FORT COLLINS, COLORADO
12 10

GIVE ANYONE WHO OFFERS TO HELP specific chores, like put a casserole in your freezer or do a load of wash. It may seem awkward at first, but accepting other people's offers takes the pressure off new parents.

—*ANNA LONDON*
MELBOURNE, AUSTRALIA
3 7M

I DROPPED MY BABY THE FIRST DAY she came home! It was a horrible feeling, but she is fine now. Smart, even.

—*JENNY B.*
NEW YORK, NEW YORK

Don't hire a baby nurse—it will just undermine your confidence as a new mom.

—*ELIZABETH LEFFERT HEISE*
CORAL GABLES, FLORIDA
3M

TELL PEOPLE SPECIFICALLY WHAT KIND OF HELP you need. Everyone thought the way to help me was to take the baby. Instead, I would have preferred help with the laundry, cleaning, paying bills, grocery shopping, cooking, grocery shopping again, and countless other tasks.

—SHEENA KROCK
KUNKLETOWN, PENNSYLVANIA
14M

INFANT INFO

During the first few weeks of life, babies can focus on objects eight to twelve inches away. At the end of the first month, most will be able to briefly focus their attention on objects as far away as three feet.

BABIES ARE NOT SWEATY AND STINKY like adults. Mostly, you just need to wash off anything they've spit up before it turns sour. A sponge bath for the first few weeks is sufficient. Too much bathing is not good for their skin.

—MARTY
CHICAGO, ILLINOIS
17 15

OUR FIRST SON DID REALLY WELL for a few weeks when we brought his baby brother home from the hospital. Then, all of a sudden, he decided that he wanted to wear diapers, too, even though he'd been potty trained for months. He also wanted to go back to a bottle, just like the baby. I worried when it persisted, but the doctor said to let him wear diapers again (I drew the line at a bottle). He said, "His friends are eventually going to notice he's wearing diapers. They'll make fun of him and it'll stop." That's exactly what happened.

—ANONYMOUS
GAMBRILLS, MARYLAND
38 36 30

EVERYONE'S A CRITIC

IF SOMEONE GIVES YOU UNSOLICITED ADVICE, ignore them.

—*ANONYMOUS*
NEW YORK, NEW YORK
9M

• • • • • • • • •

LITTLE OLD LADIES ALWAYS THOUGHT MY SON LOOKED COLD no matter how bundled up he was. I just smiled patiently. I figure one day I'll be the little old lady dispensing advice just for an excuse to come fuss over a baby!

—*DAWN*
COLUMBUS, OHIO
7 4M

• • • • • • • • •

UNSOLICITED COMMENTS ABOUT YOUR BABY can seem presumptuous, but sometimes a stranger can notice things that you might not. One time a woman on the bus told me that my son was very observant, saying, "That kid's taking in everything." She noticed what a genius my son was before I did!

—*JOAN*
NEW YORK, NEW YORK
32

BABY'S BEST FRIEND

ALWAYS SUPERVISE PETS WITH A BABY. Even the most trusted pet can accidentally harm a child. We put a screen door on the bedroom which allowed us to hear our daughter if she cried, and let fresh air circulate, while not letting our cat have access to the baby's room.

—*Erin Brown Conroy*
Schoolcraft, Michigan

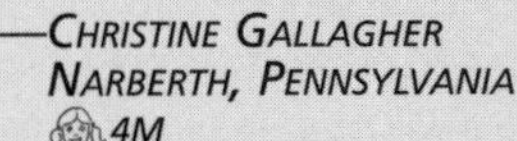

WHEN MY DAUGHTER WAS BORN, we rubbed a blanket all over her and took it home for the dog to smell and play with. That way, when she came home, our dog wasn't sniffing her and going crazy with a new person in our home.

—*Christine Gallagher*
Narberth, Pennsylvania
4M

WHEN THE BABY CAME HOME, OUR CAT STARTED having real territorial problems and started spraying in every room. He sprayed all over the baby's toys! We tried a number of things to help him, including hiring a cat "therapist" who advised giving him antidepressants. We ended up giving our cat away.

—*A.C.*
South Portland, Maine
5

I WAS ALWAYS TOLD TO SMEAR PEANUT BUTTER on a new baby's toes and let the dog lick it off. (Not too much peanut butter, mind you, or the dog might forget there are toes under there!) I passed this advice on to my sons when they had kids of their own, and they said it worked like a charm.

—*Vera Petty*
Beaumont, Texas

I'D HEARD THAT CATS SOMETIMES LEAP INTO A BABY'S CRIB and hurt the baby, so we kept a careful eye on our two cats. In turn they kept an eye on the baby. We have pictures of each cat sitting on the windowsill studying the baby as if they were keeping watch over him. I actually think Ficha and Fuzzy took the baby in stride better than we did.

—LINDA ANDREWS REEVES
SAN ANTONIO, TEXAS
10 5

• • • • • • • •

A DOG TRAINER ONCE TOLD US THAT THE FIRST YEAR, you protect the baby from the dog. But once your child starts to walk, you need to protect the dog from the baby.

—SUE RODMAN
ATLANTA, GEORGIA
6 4

• • • • • • • •

OUR CAT WAS A KITTEN WHEN OUR BABY WAS BORN so really they grew up together. That's the best way to avoid jealousy on the kid's or pet's part!

—BEV PORTER
COLORADO SPRINGS, COLORADO
14 11

• • • • • • • •

WITH OUR FIRST SON, OUR DOG ACTUALLY SAT IN THE CORNER for about two weeks, pouting. We made sure to pet her and play with her while holding our son, so she knew that he wasn't taking all her attention away, and we tried to keep her on her usual schedule so she wouldn't think we forgot her. Gradually the dog came around and now they are the best of friends.

—MICHELLE M.
OOSTBURG, WISCONSIN
2 2M

DOUBLE YOUR FUN

IF YOU HAVE TWINS, PLEASE, FOR THE LOVE OF GOD, don't dress them identically.

—BETTY SMITH
PITTSBURGH, PENNSYLVANIA

• • • • • • • •

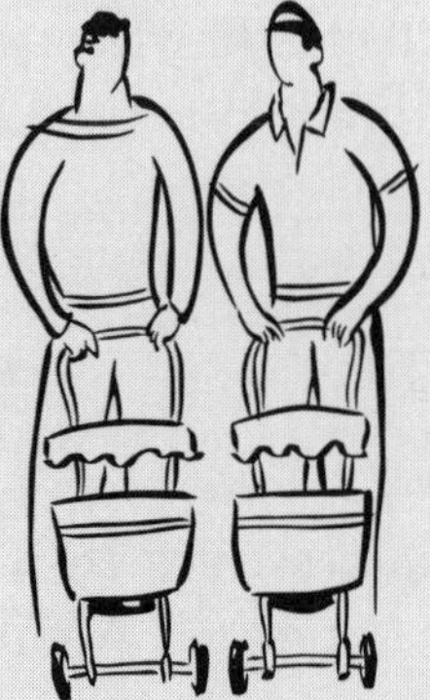

WHEN YOU HAVE TWINS, you're going to get advice and comments from all sorts of people—solicited and unsolicited—and from other people who have twins.

—M.J.W.
KIRKLAND, WASHINGTON
-1

• • • • • • • •

TWINS SHARE A SPECIAL BOND. Let them sleep in the same crib. Even as newborns our twins needed to be together. If we laid them down on opposite ends of the crib they'd end up with their feet touching each other. If they didn't feel each other they'd start crying.

—PAM BOEA
SYRACUSE, NEW YORK
19 17 -15 12

• • • • • • • •

HAVING TWINS WAS A LOT EASIER THAN HAVING ONE CHILD. Twins amuse each other from a very young age. With a single child, you spend a lot more time trying to keep them happy.

—KELLY DIXON
KIRKLAND, WASHINGTON
23 -16

MOTHER REALLY DOES KNOW BEST—*your* mother that is! I didn't listen to any of my mother's suggestions for things to buy the baby and she ended up being right. The stroller she bought to keep at her house was nicer, the baby preferred the swing she picked for her house. He even seemed to like the toys she picked more, too. Now I listen when my mom tells me what to buy.

—*BRYNN CYNOR*
BUFFALO GROVE, ILLINOIS
1

DON'T BOTHER WITH FANCY BATHTUBS for your newborn. Babies are so tiny, all they need is a little plastic tub or the sink itself. I recommend always having your baby sit on a washcloth to help prevent slipping. Babies are very, very slippery!

—*JENNY W.*
NEW YORK, NEW YORK
4

WE SHOULD HAVE REALIZED THAT the personality differences between our parents/in-laws and us would not disappear with the bliss of cuddling cute little babies. On the contrary, the differences became heightened in the face of total sleep deprivation and crying, colic-stricken babies, and this created stress on top of stress. When the grandparents are only visiting to hold and feed one of the babies during daytime hours, this really does little to help the parents. The grandparents, of twin grand-babies especially, should be prepared to help with the cooking, cleaning, and even nighttime duty if their visit is meant to be any relief to the parents.

—*A.A.*
CONNECTICUT

3

For the first month or so I found myself really looking forward to my daughter falling asleep. I would panic when she was awake.

—*CYNTHIA*
PORTLAND, MAINE
2

Parenting certainly expanded me. It questioned me. It challenged me. It's a new kind of love.

—*Marion Roach*
Troy, New York
8

The first time I gave my daughter a bath, I almost drowned her. She was in her little baby tub, and I was so exhausted that I must have relaxed my elbow, and my baby's face went under the water. Thank goodness, my husband noticed, yelled, and I pulled our baby's head out of the water. She did some sputtering, but she was just fine.

—*Rosana*
New York, New York

• • • • • • • • •

My mother was a godsend in helping me get sleep because she stays up late and gets up early. If I was tired or awakened early and felt too sleepy to handle the baby, my mother would already be up and waiting when I took the baby to her.

—*Monica and Todd Dennis*
Bridgeport, Connecticut
4 6M

• • • • • • • • •

Since having a baby, starting a conversation between me and my husband is difficult because we're either too busy or too tired. I miss having conversations with my husband so now we're making an effort to talk while the baby sleeps.

—*Camille Fredrickson*
Brussels, Belgium
4.5M

• • • • • • • • •

I was a notorious procrastinator. No more. Now, if I have four hours to work, that's it. It's to get done then. I've also learned to accept things as "good enough." Very hard, since I was a perfectionist.

—*Britt Stromberg*
Camano Island, Washington
11M

HOW MOTHERHOOD CHANGED ME

I GREW UP WHEN I HAD A BABY. I used to be "wild," but as a mother I felt I needed to be a responsible adult. Sometimes I miss the old times, but as long as my children are small I feel that I need to be available and fully functioning at all times.

—HEIDE A.W. KAMINSKI
TECUMSEH, MICHIGAN
18 15 6

• • • • • • • •

HAVING A BABY MADE ME MUCH MORE conservative in my actions. I took fewer personal risks. I became more interested in politics and society, as I wanted to have a good society for her to live in. I became more involved with my extended family. I thought more about the choices I made to set a good example for her. I also worried a lot more.

—CLAIRE YURDIN
SEATTLE, WASHINGTON
26

• • • • • • • •

THE OTHER NIGHT, OUR FRIENDS WERE HEADING into the city for an art opening, and there I was, waving goodbye—barefoot, in my sundress, one boob out, and a child hanging on me! I'm in a very different place now than I was before.

—M. DEJONG
FAIRFAX, CALIFORNIA
5W

• • • • • • • •

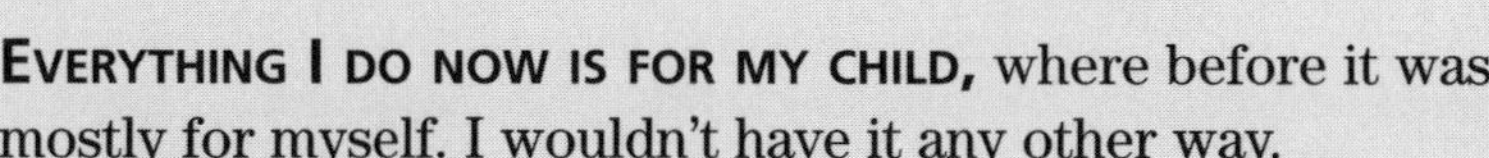

EVERYTHING I DO NOW IS FOR MY CHILD, where before it was mostly for myself. I wouldn't have it any other way.

—P.J.
HAVRE DE GRACE, MARYLAND
2

DRESS FOR SUCCESS

I HAVE A GRIEVANCE ABOUT THE SNAPS. When you are so sleep-deprived and your baby is kicking and screaming, it is the hardest thing in the world to get those snaps inside the leg to line up properly! They should be color coded, to help ensure proper matching and reduce frustration.

—K.H.
FAIRFAX, CALIFORNIA
5.5M

• • • • • • • • •

I'M WONDERING IF IT'S POSSIBLE FOR BABY CLOTHING designers to make it more difficult to dress and undress a baby. Buttons? Are you kidding? On a squirmy baby? And 57 snaps for one pair of bottoms? Or how about the full-body suit? Whose bright idea was that for poopy baby? It's like a practical joke. As I struggled with my babies' clothing while they cried and tried to wriggle free, I kept thinking a TV host would pop out and yell, "Gotcha! We were secretly videotaping you to see just how ridiculous you'd look trying to fasten 27 hook-buttons, a line of Velcro and all those snaps." Unfortunately, that never happened.

—JWAIII
ATLANTA, GEORGIA
5 2

• • • • • • • • •

MAKE SURE TO DRESS YOUR BABY IN DORKY LITTLE CLOTHES with silly bunny ears and tails and that sort of thing. It's the only time in your life you'll have such complete control over what they wear, and it's funny! We took pictures and now that they're teens, it's great to break out the photos and embarrass them.

—JILL H.
NEW YORK, NEW YORK
14 12

BEFORE MY FIRST CHILD WAS BORN, I was working full-time. I thought I'd keep working and get my master's degree, too, with the baby just "fitting in." After the baby was born, everything changed. I hadn't counted on falling in love with this little person and wanting to spend all my time with the baby!

—*ANDREA LARSON*
FORT COLLINS, COLORADO
12 9

I did not take enough time off when I left the hospital. I needed more time to bond and rest before working again.

—*DAWN RODRIGUEZ*
PASSAIC, NEW JERSEY

• • • • • • • •

MAKE YOUR CHILD AN ACTIVE PART of your lifestyle. You might not realize that they actually like going to the bank or the grocery store with you. Take the baby with you because not only will it make your life easier, you'll get in some serious bonding time.

—*TESS DIXON*
CORALVILLE, IOWA
4 17M

• • • • • • • •

SHARING WORK WAS DIVIDE-AND-CONQUER with a baby in the house. She cooks. He cleans. She does laundry. He does dishes. He does it his way. She does it hers. No questions, as long as it gets done. In our house Dad does baths. Dad reads. Dad puts the kids to bed. This is "daddy time." Mom feeds at night and Dad does the rest (dressing, bathing, diapers, singing, etc.).

—*JUDITH WONG*
MILWAUKEE, WISCONSIN
5 2 4M

• • • • • • • •

BUY A SLING! Women have been carrying babies across their chests for centuries.

—*DENISE*
JASPER, INDIANA
9 6 1

NECESSARY OBJECTS

DON'T BUY CUTE COVERS FOR THE CHANGING PADS. It's so much easier when you can just wipe down the pad itself, which has a plastic exterior.

—TONY T.
SAN FRANCISCO, CALIFORNIA
6M

• • • • • • • •

I WOULD ADVISE PARENTS TO NOT WASTE MONEY on things like bassinettes and fancy crib bumpers when they won't get used for long, if at all. Our son insists on sleeping with us for at least half the night, and he always has, so we could have saved ourselves $300 and purchased a used crib instead of a fancy new one.

—DEANN ROSSETTI
MAPLE VALLEY, WASHINGTON
4

• • • • • • • •

THE ONE THING YOU ALWAYS NEED to have with you is a plastic bag. In fact, you should have a stash of them in the stroller, car, and your bag. You never know when you'll need to bag up a dirty diaper, smelly bib, or half-eaten banana. They're especially useful when you're on a plane and your seat is covered in garbage.

—LORI B.
CHARLESTON, SOUTH CAROLINA
19 16 13 3

• • • • • • • •

YOU SHOULD DEFINITELY BUY A SWING-O-MATIC, because when the baby is crying and nothing makes the baby happy, the Swing-O-Matic will. It is kind of depressing because the baby likes the Swing-O-Matic better than you! But you'll get over that.

—BILL W.
SEATTLE, WASHINGTON
26 23

I RECOMMEND BUYING TWO COVERS FOR YOUR CHANGING PAD, even if you think you can do without. This way you can have one in the wash and use the other.

—*CAROL GILMORE*
EASTON, PENNSYLVANIA
6

EVERY MOTHER NEEDS TO HAVE A BABY SWING. We call it the Neglect-O-Matic.

—*SHARON LONDON*
SAN FRANCISCO, CALIFORNIA
42 40

HAVE A SWING. BABIES LIKE TO SWING. It gives parents a chance to do other things.

—*S.S.*
VIRGINIA BEACH, VIRGINIA
8

BUY A BABY CARRIER, SPECIFICALLY A BABY BJORN. This is absolutely the best one compared to some of the cheaper ones. It's more comfortable, and the straps in the back crisscross for better support.

—*KELLY POLAND*
FORT COLLINS, COLORADO
6W

MY FAVORITE PIECE OF BABY EQUIPMENT IS CLOTH DIAPERS, not for diapering the baby but for bleachable cleaning up of unspeakable baby messes.

—*MELODY PHILLIPS*
SARATOGA SPRINGS, NEW YORK
17 16

FOR YOUR BABY'S SAKE, SLOW DOWN for at least the first six months. With our first child, I had the attitude that nothing in my life needed to change—we could still do all the things we did before. And we did. But it wasn't so good for the baby. By the second child, I learned to slow down and adjust to the baby's schedule. You just have to accept that this is a phase and remember that it won't last forever.

—LISA
WINDSOR, COLORADO
16 13

Get a stroller that's practical. Specifically, look for one that isn't too bulky when folded.

—DAVID
SYRACUSE, NEW YORK
6 4

SLINGS ARE THE GREATEST INVENTION for the crucial "fourth trimester." I wore my daughter six to eight hours a day. Whenever my daughter would cry, I'd stick her in the sling and walk around. She'd usually go to sleep.

—BRITT STROMBERG
CAMANO ISLAND, WASHINGTON
11M

THE BABY SLING REALLY HELPED OUR SON SLEEP, which let us get a lot more done. This isn't possible with the Bjorn or front carriers. The only problem is that slings need to be made in father-friendly colors. At first I didn't want to wear one because they either looked too hippie or too girlie. But I've learned that if it works, you wear it. If it's pink, you wear it. It'll have throw-up on it sooner or later anyway.

—GUY ADAMSON
CONNECTICUT
14M

OH, HOW I LOVED THAT SLING! I'd tuck my son in there and we'd walk all over, trying not to chuckle at all the other moms maneuvering bulky strollers through tiny store aisles. My son loved it because he was up at my height, he could see everything and hear me clearly when I talked to him, and it freed up my arms to hold my husband's hand, carry objects, pick things up, etc.

—STEPHANIE WOLFE
GROTON, CONNECTICUT
23M

PLACE YOUR BABY TO NAP IN A BABY SWING when you need to take a shower (within your eyesight, of course). Both baby and parent will feel rested and better.

—C. KARP
IRVINE, CALIFORNIA
4

ACCEPT ALL THE ASSISTANCE YOU CAN GET. As long as you show appreciation, the grandparents don't mind helping.

—SUETTA GRIFFITH
FISHERSVILLE, VIRGINIA
33 31

"SHOPPING" MEANS BUYING THE SAME dress in four different colors before your little one cries, wets herself, gets tired or—by age one—tries to climb out of the stroller.

—CASSANDRA FOX
FAIRFAX STATION, VIRGINIA
18 15

Don't let your compulsion to do everything perfectly turn you into someone who tries to do it all alone. I wish I could have found, and accepted, more help.

—NANCY ENGLISH
PORTLAND, MAINE

Babies are wiggly little things and need neck and head support all the time, so don't underestimate that!

—*Jenny B.*
New York, New York

If you're a young couple and you're having a baby, don't be concerned about your house looking perfect. Your baby doesn't care how your house looks.

—*Nora Hammond*
Louisville, Kentucky
39 35

• • • • • • • •

Before I brought the baby home, I wish I had known not to take myself too seriously.

—*Marion Roach*
Troy, New York

• • • • • • • •

You see yourselves as "partners" before the kids come, but afterwards we became one mom and one dad with distinct roles.

—*Deana Krause*
Chicago, Illinois
11 9

• • • • • • • •

Take the day off after your child gets his first immunizations.

—*Jonathan and Juliana Rollins*
Marietta, Georgia
11W

5 The Ultimate Choice: Breastfeeding or Formula

Is breast best? Or should baby be on the bottle? Few issues of early babyhood engender such strong emotions as the decision whether or not to breastfeed. There are convincing arguments for both sides, so the choice isn't easy. Ultimately, it's up to the new parents. Here we present points and counterpoints, and we throw in some unique tips that will help you with every feeding.

WHEN NURSING YOUR BABY, no matter where you are or what you're doing, try to look right into those precious eyes and savor the moment. That bond is something which will last forever.

—*BRIGITTE THOMPSON*
10 6 2

BREASTFEEDING IS UNLIKE ANY OTHER BOND—SO MUCH STEMS FROM THE EMOTION ALONE.

—*DENISE JASPER, INDIANA*
9 6 1

YOU DON'T HAVE TO BREASTFEED if you don't want to. Your child will survive, and you will, too.

—*L.S.*
SHARON, MASSACHUSETTS
5 4

I RECOMMEND THAT EXPECTANT PARENTS READ up on nursing, and maybe even keep the number of the local La Leche League handy. I really studied up on the whole pregnancy and childbirth thing but for some reason I thought nursing would be a no-brainer. Wrong! My first son had problems feeding. As an exhausted first-time mom it was especially hard to deal with.

—*VICKY MLYNIEC*
LOS GATOS, CALIFORNIA
19 15

I PRACTICED BREASTFEEDING AT HOME with some really good friends over before I tried nursing in public. I figured if I accidentally flashed them or just got flustered, we could all laugh about it.

—*DENISE*
BOSTON, MASSACHUSETTS
4 1

I BREASTFED FOR THE FIRST YEAR AND LOVED IT. It allowed me to develop a relationship with my baby that wouldn't have been achieved with formula or pumping. It also gave her the necessary nutrients and antibodies she needed that only I could give.

—*E. HIRSH*
WEST PALM BEACH, FLORIDA
7

I RECOMMEND BREASTFEEDING FOR THE FIRST YEAR. Why? I lost my pregnancy weight faster. I don't get my period while I'm breastfeeding. My son rarely gets sick because it's boosted his immune system. It's free. It's always available when my baby is hungry. My baby never smelled like formula. And breast milk is what human babies are meant to eat!

—*MICHELLE BELT*
EDGEWATER, MARYLAND
4 3M

"Use formula to supplement breastfeeding. It gives you a break."

—*JESSICA VAUGHAN*
RANDOLPH, VERMONT
10 8 6 4

IN THE BEGINNING, BREASTFEEDING HURTS. It hurts, it hurts. Your nipples are sore, crusty, bloody, and for the first few weeks they feel like they are going to fall off. Even though the books say the baby has to be sucking the right way and latch on and all that crap, it doesn't matter. Your breasts have never had the likes of a baby's suck on it, no matter what strange boyfriends you may have had in the past. If you really want to breastfeed, grin and bear it and it will get better. It's all worth it in the end.

—*ANONYMOUS*
SINGER ISLAND, FLORIDA
1

Make sure you have a good pump—don't be stingy!—so that you're not always bound to the baby.

—*ANONYMOUS*
AUSTIN, TEXAS
6

STRONG WORDS

DO YOUR RESEARCH ON THE BENEFITS OF BREASTFEEDING. Everyone talks about it being a "choice," but if you spend a moment comparing formula to breast milk, there is no contest. To give a child formula is almost criminal considering it contains so many harmful preservatives, is so difficult for a tiny baby to digest, and does not build your child's immune system.

—ELIZABETH LEFFERT HEISE
CORAL GABLES, FLORIDA
3M

DON'T BE AFRAID TO ADMIT THAT YOU DON'T WANT to have a child attached to your breast 24/7. If it were as natural as everybody tells you it is, why are there "lactation consultants" on every maternity floor just waiting to force your breast repeatedly into your newborn's mouth to teach him/her how to "latch on?" If it were natural, he/she would come out knowing how to nurse.

—ANONYMOUS
BROOKLYN, NEW YORK
2

THE FIRST COUPLE OF WEEKS OF BREASTFEEDING really hurt. I mean really. So make a pact to stick it out for three weeks to a month. Then, if you still hate it, you can always switch to bottles. But most likely, you'll have gotten past the bad period and will start to appreciate how convenient it is, and what a great chance it is to comfort, feed, and bond at the same time.

—*K.T.*
BURLINGTON, VERMONT
5 4 1

• • • • • • • •

I WAS AGAINST BREASTFEEDING. I thought it was so gross to have another human being latched on all the time. Then I became pregnant and all of a sudden I was all about breastfeeding. I became a huge advocate for it and encouraged all my family and friends to breastfeed. I have no idea what changed my mind . . . maybe the hormones!

—*LESLIE BUNDY*
WAUKESHA, WISCONSIN
1

• • • • • • • •

I HAD TROUBLE NURSING MY NEWBORN because I was not producing enough milk. I remember calling a lactation consultant and was told to keep trying, drink lots of water, eat well, and get plenty of rest (yeah, right). By the time my son went for his one-month visit, he was on the lowest end of the scale for weight gain. I tried the same routine for a few more weeks. My son was miserable at every nursing. I was a mess. We would both cry through it. I finally decided and put him on formula. What a world of difference! He was gaining weight well and we were both happy at feedings. It was like I had a whole new baby!

—*SHEENA KROCK*
KUNKLETOWN, PENNSYLVANIA
14M

People become much more tolerant of nursing in public once they hear the baby screaming for a few minutes.

—*RACHEL RUVO*
CHAPEL HILL, NORTH CAROLINA

IF YOU INTEND TO BREASTFEED, line up a lactation consultant before you give birth—get tips beforehand and attend a breastfeeding support group. I assumed it would all "come naturally," but it's not easy. I was up 24 hours a day with sore everything until I found a lactation consultant who saved my little family!

—*ELIZABETH LEFFERT HEISE*
CORAL GABLES, FLORIDA
3M

"Breastfeeding is very hard at first, but it's wonderful in the long run. Pregnant women should be told about the health benefits of breastfeeding—for baby and for mother."

—*MARRIT INGMAN*
AUSTIN, TEXAS
2

You hear that breast milk doesn't stain—it does.

—*MARYBETH*
SAN FRANCISCO, CALIFORNIA
4

FORMULA ISN'T POISON, despite what some women say. I fed my son my breast milk for almost six months, but then switched to formula. My son is now a perfectly healthy, happy and smart four-year-old. He is perfect—tall for his age, lean and lanky, smart and healthy.

—*DEANN ROSSETTI*
MAPLE VALLEY, WASHINGTON
4

FROM THE SIDELINES

SMART HUSBANDS SHOULD URGE THEIR WIVES TO CONTINUE nursing for as long as possible, because as long as they're nursing they're the only ones who can deal with nighttime feedings. As far as I'm concerned, kids can continue to nurse until they're 18 years old.

—Joel Rosenfeld
New York, New York
-17 15

IF THE WIFE'S IN CHARGE OF INPUT, the husband's in charge of output!

—Judy Conners
Wichita, Kansas
40 37 34

I'M AGAINST NURSING. I think it's important to share all those fun and not-so-fun responsibilities. I liked getting up in the middle of the night, changing diapers, watching them sleep, babysitting and caring for them. I would've been disappointed not to have had those opportunities.

—Ken Blaise
Diablo, California
26

MY WIFE BREASTFED, would not pump, and did not want to feed the baby formula. I felt helpless at times, and I was concerned the baby didn't know who I was. Then I realized that I was there to read, go on walks, play, and make faces. Now, at a year old, our daughter still fusses almost every time my wife changes or feeds her. With me, everything is a game to her—she is good as gold and laughs when I take care of her.

—Marc A. Claybon
Golden, Colorado
15M

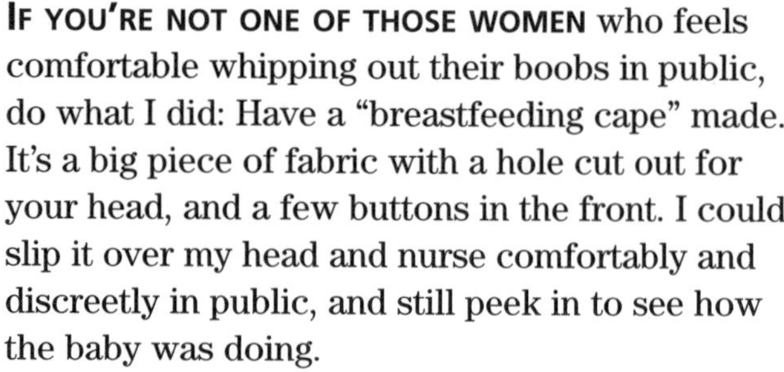

IF YOU'RE NOT ONE OF THOSE WOMEN who feels comfortable whipping out their boobs in public, do what I did: Have a "breastfeeding cape" made. It's a big piece of fabric with a hole cut out for your head, and a few buttons in the front. I could slip it over my head and nurse comfortably and discreetly in public, and still peek in to see how the baby was doing.

—*ANONYMOUS*
CHARLESTON, SOUTH CAROLINA
5

• • • • • • • •

I CALLED A LACTACTON CONSULTANT FOR ADVICE when I was fretting about how to breastfeed my triplets. She said to take out a calendar, call everyone you know and get people to come over and help you every day because you can't do it by yourself. I had women coming over from my church that I had never met! It was the best advice anyone could have given me because for the first three months I was feeding babies every 30 minutes, 24/7.

—*CHRISTIE PATRICK*
ATLANTA, GEORGIA
- - 8M

INFANT INFO

Studies show that breastfed babies are less likely to be under- or overweight and are less susceptible to disease than formula-fed babies.

• • • • • • • •

THIS IS THE BEST ADVICE I GOT ABOUT FEEDING twins: First, if you are breastfeeding, assign one breast to each child and always stick with that.

Second, when one wakes up, always wake the other up and feed them at the same time. This helps to get them on a schedule.

Third, when they are on solid food, just use one spoon for the both of them. One bite for this one, then one bite for that one.

—*CELINE SWANSON*
KIRKLAND, WASHINGTON
10 - 6

WAYS TO WEAN

WEAN YOUR CHILDREN EARLY. It's much harder the longer you wait. My daughter is two and a half and I have been unable to stop nursing, even though I want to. I thought, in the very beginning, she and I would know together when it was time to stop. Now I want my body back; I'm physically ready but she's not emotionally ready.

—*CYNTHIA*
PORTLAND, MAINE
2

• • • • • • • •

I TIMED MY BREASTFEEDING TO STOP when I went back to work. I have a job that means I am in a lot of meetings so I can't always get away to pump. I made sure I started weaning before I went back to work, not after.

—*JULIE KIND*
ARLINGTON, VIRGINIA
6M

• • • • • • • •

WHEN YOU'RE WEANING A BABY FROM NURSING, it's the night feedings that are hardest to stop.

—*K.B.*
SAN FRANCISCO, CALIFORNIA
6 3 3M

• • • • • • • •

I BREASTFED, BUT I DID NOT HAVE ENOUGH MILK to feed her completely, so I combined breastfeeding and bottle-feeding, which worked well for us. She weaned herself from the breast and then continued with the bottle alone.

—*CLAIRE YURDIN*
SEATTLE, WASHINGTON
26

Breast pumps don't work! I tried both battery-powered and manual pumps. I sprayed milk all over the room!

—*M.S.*
Toronto, Canada
11 9 7

NURSING IS THE GREATEST SURVIVAL TOOL to parenting and the best thing you can do for your baby. I loved the sensuality and closeness of it and the ability to comfort my child.

—*Jennifer Taylor Atanda*
Alexandria, Virginia
2

• • • • • • • • •

BOTTLED MILK CAN BE SERVED at room temperature—it doesn't need to be heated on the stove or in the microwave. Each night, we'd put three batches of formula on a tray, along with three bottles already filled with liners and water. When our daughter woke up, we dumped one batch of formula into the bottle, shook it up, and were ready to go. It saved all that time of going downstairs and heating up the bottle, so all of us could go back to sleep that much sooner.

—*Gail Manginelli*
Scottsdale, Arizona

• • • • • • • • •

I CAN DISTILL MOTHERHOOD DOWN TO ONE LINE: When in doubt, nurse; if that doesn't work, give Tylenol (once the doctor says it's OK, of course).

—*Rachel Ruvo*
Chapel Hill, North Carolina

6 Diaper Patrol: Getting to the Bottom of Things

Diapers. For many, the mere mention of the word comes with a horror film soundtrack (the distressing strains from "Psycho," anyone?). But this particular aspect of "baby-rearing" doesn't have to be scary business. If you're prepared with the weapon of knowledge, it's at least a little less frightening to open the door into a whole new world of horrific sights and smells. Bottoms up!

MY HUSBAND AND I HAVE A GAME. The last person to put a finger to his or her nose has to change the diaper. We've found our hand-nose coordination has really sharpened the last few years.

—*ALEXIS KLEINHANS*

DISPOSABLE DIAPERS ARE A GIFT FROM HEAVEN.

—*KATHY PENTON*
SAVANNAH, GEORGIA
23

GIRLS HAVE LOTS OF NOOKS AND CRANNIES; they're like an English muffin. There's a zillion folds in there. With boys, when the air hits them, they pee. So, as soon you open the diaper, you drop a tissue on him and cover it up.

—*EDDIE FINKELSTEIN*
CHAPPAQUA, NEW YORK
16 14 9

Get a hair dryer. If you use a hair dryer after you change a diaper and wipe the baby down, there is no diaper rash.

—*WILLEM KNIBBE*
ALAMEDA, CALIFORNIA
7M

• • • • • • • •

MY HUSBAND COULDN'T STAND to hear the baby cry, ever. When he changed our son's diapers, he would put on those safety earmuffs that you wear when you're using power tools. He wore those for the first six months. However, those did not protect him one bit from getting a pee shot right in face.

—*MARET VAN FLEET*
ELLICOT CITY, MARYLAND
8 6

• • • • • • • •

NO MATTER WHAT SOMEONE—and that someone will likely be your mother-in-law—says, don't ever stick your finger in a baby's diaper to see if it's dirty. I tried it and got a nasty surprise. It's far better to take the time to unsnap all the snaps on their outfit.

—*RUSSELL LISSAU*
ARLINGTON HEIGHTS, ILLINOIS
2

• • • • • • • •

FOR BOYS, REMEMBER TO ALWAYS, I mean *always*, have a diaper cloth, burp rag, towel, or clothes from the hamper in your hand during the diaper change. I got sprayed a few times before I learned that lesson.

—*C.H.*
LOS ANGELES, CALIFORNIA
6 4 1

THERE ARE SOME DISPOSABLE DIAPERS, like Tushies, that aren't made with all those artificial chemicals and plastic by-products against the baby's skin. I think it has cut down on rashes. It just seems more natural and better for her than the other ones.

—*CARL M.*
MINNEAPOLIS, MINNESOTA
1

"Changing a diaper isn't brain surgery. Men have a tendency to make things harder than they really are. Just lay the baby down, untape the diaper and wipe them clean. Put a new one on and voila! You're done!"

—*STEVEN GREEN*
LOS ANGELES, CALIFORNIA
35 30 29 25 17

COMPLAIN ALL YOU WANT about having to change diapers, but I am grateful to be a mom after the invention of disposable diapers. My own mother had to use safety pins on cloth diapers that she had to launder herself. Now *that's* something to complain about.

—*MISSY*
DETROIT, MICHIGAN
14 12 9

Poop. Get used to it. It becomes part of your life, and conversation about it lasts a lot longer than you want.

—*ALEXIS KLEINHANS*

YOUR FIRST DIAPER

Changing your first dirty diaper can easily become one of those sweaty, tension-filled, bomb-defusing situations in which you're yelling for your spouse to help but he can't hear because the baby's wailing at the top of its lungs and your hands are shaking and there's runny yellow poop all over the half-unsnapped onesie, and the baby's face is turning purple and you don't know yet that that's what babies look like when they poop.

Just keep this in mind: Nothing is as frightening as that initial poopy diaper and in no time at all you become so unfazed by this, and a whole lot more.

—*Kristen Ramsey*
Los Angeles, California
3

The first time babies expel feces, they do it in a big way. My newborn daughter's nurse warned me that it might take her a while to start going to the bathroom because she wasn't lubricated yet. Two days later...well, it was like Niagara Falls! I guess things had really backed up! My biggest mistake is that I had put her in cloth diapers. I should've made sure she was sealed up really good, like with disposables AND plastic pants.

—*Rachel Walaskay*
Sedalia, Colorado
11 8

TRY USING CLOTH DIAPERS DURING THE DAY, and disposables at night. Cloth diapers are better for the environment, and they are no more expensive or difficult than disposables. They are better for the baby, too, because he or she will only have cotton against their skin and not that plastic-y, chemically stuff. Plus a cloth diaper service will deliver clean diapers and pick up the dirties.

—*SAM*
SANTA MONICA, CALIFORNIA
13 1

We should be lobbying for a diaper recycling program.

—*ISABELLA BAUHAUS*
SANTA CRUZ, CALIFORNIA
18M

"I can't imagine how older generations made it without disposable diapers. I know they're bad for the environment, but they save oodles of time and make this job much more bearable."

—*DAVE BAUDER*
CROTON-ON-HUDSON, NEW YORK
5 3

KEEP SPARE DIAPERS IN A FEW PLACES, not just your diaper bag. Diapers are small, so I just put one in my regular purse, one in the glove compartment, one in my husband's computer bag for work, one in the stroller pocket. These emergency stashes have come in handy a couple times.

—*CHRISTINE B.*
NEW YORK, NEW YORK
4M

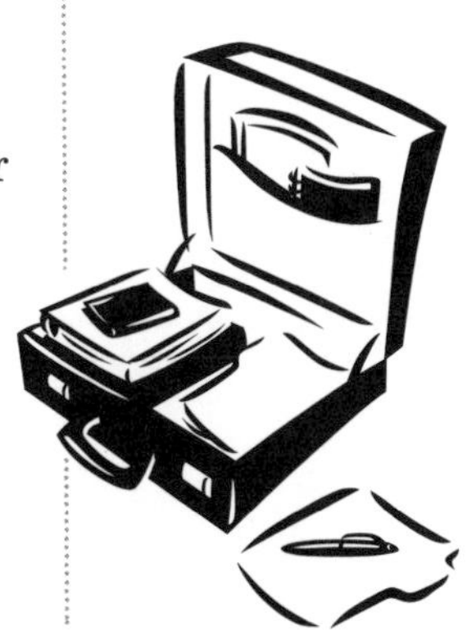

AFTER GIVING BIRTH TO MY SON, my friend was with me at the hospital, and she helped me change his diaper for the first time. As soon as he had his diaper off he started to pee. I was so surprised that I picked him up carried him around the room, asking my friend, "What do I do?!" Needless to say I made a big mess. That's when the nurse walked in and said, "Ladies, when you're changing his diaper, have a clean diaper ready to cover his penis."

—SARAH GOLDBERG
SOUTH PORTLAND, MAINE
16 8

• • • • • • • •

Learn how to diaper a baby the "normal" way and also in a face-down position. When they start crawling around, this skill comes in handy.

—C.H.
LOS ANGELES, CALIFORNIA
6 4 1

IF YOU SHOW EXTREME ENTHUSIASM for changing a diaper, your baby will appreciate it and you'll have fun, too. I made up a song to sing to my daughter whenever it was my turn to change her diaper. When my daughter was older and more alert, she'd start singing the song with me. It made diaper changing so much more efficient, because she was distracted by the song (and my singing). When my son was born, we sang the song to him. "The Poopy Diaper Song," as it became known, is now a part of family lore.

—JWAIII
ATLANTA, GEORGIA
5 2

• • • • • • • •

RATHER THAN CARRYING DIAPER changing supplies around the house, create diaper "stations." I put a basket with two or three diapers, wipes, and ointment in every room of my house. Literally every room—the dining room, living room, master bedroom. This way, I didn't have to lug things around, and changing diapers didn't become an interruption.

—JEANNIE SPONHEIM
LOVELAND, COLORADO

FOR HYPER CHILDREN, take the following steps while changing diapers:
1. Have all your supplies ready.
2. Before the diaper is off, have a big wad of wipes at hand.
3. Give the baby a favorite toy to hold on to (this will keep her attention for about five seconds).

This will help you restrain the baby long enough to clean off as much of the mess as possible. Of course, you may still have to chase her around bare-bottomed to get the clean diaper on!

—JULIE BAJUSZ
SAN ANTONIO, TEXAS
7 5

Dads should get involved in the down and dirty of bathing and diapers. For a male, the learning curve is a lot steeper.

—IAN WHITEHEAD
CANYON LAKE, TEXAS
25 24
- 23 11

BE PREPARED

Murphy's Law: The worst diaper emergencies occur when you are least prepared to deal with them. If you think you can slip in a five-minute trip to the store without the diaper bag, or go anywhere and forget the diaper bag, that's when disaster will surely strike.

Create an emergency kit for the car (extra diapers, lots of wipes, a blanket that you don't mind getting dirty and lots of extra plastic bags for disposal). Remember, you can never have enough diapers. If you think you'll need three, take five.

—KEITH REGAN
GRAFTON, MASSACHUSETTS
5 3

While one can describe the nastiness of meconium, one really has to experience it to get the full effect.

—*Tim Newell*
Houston, Texas
5M

Cloth diapers seem like a great idea because they are wonderful for the environment. The problem is, you have to buy the wraps which are very expensive. Plus, washing them, even if you use a diaper service, is very time consuming.

—*Isabella Bauhaus*
Santa Cruz, California
18M

Buy the right diaper bag. It's worth the money, considering you're going to be carrying it for a year or two. And some of them look so great that you can use them as carry-ons later.

—*Dawn*
Columbus, Ohio
7 4M

"Always keep a change of clothes for yourself and baby, especially during the baby's first year when messes (and leaks!) are more likely to occur."

—*J.L.*
Miami, Florida
6

Diaper Genies are great but the refills are expensive. Buy a separate trash can and cheap liners (from Costco) for those pee-pee diapers and throw the liners out every other day. Use the diaper genie for the stinky poo-poo diapers.

—*Anonymous*
Austin, Texas
21M

MY NEPHEW'S DIRTY DIAPERS WERE THE MOST powerfully overwhelming, repugnant things I have ever encountered. One night while babysitting, I was changing him in the bathroom, and had him in the tub for thorough cleaning. I had the bathroom window open so I could breathe a little, and suddenly my husband came running in the room, took the dirty diaper and sailed it out the window. He said, "I'm sorry, honey, I just couldn't have that thing in the house one more second." So I had to go find it and put it in an outside trashcan.

—*KATHY PENTON*
SAVANNAH, GEORGIA
23

Babies have perfect skin naturally and smell delicious—well, once the crap is cleaned off of them.

—*SAM*
SANTA MONICA, CALIFORNIA
13 1

USE THE FORCE

Gentlemen, heed my advice: Be the Diaper Jedi. To begin, master the dual leg lift—with one hand, grasp both ankles in a single clutch. Fold the front of the diaper back over the poop to create an absorbent but temporary workspace under the baby's dirty, wiggly butt. Wipe the area clean, leaving nothing behind. If your station is properly set up, a tube of rash cream is on hand, ready to go. With practice, you'll flip the cap and squeeze a dab on your finger with the flair of lighting a Zippo. All the while you are singing out loud, distracting the kid. A new song every time. File away the favorites for "code red" situations when your newborn turns into a kicking, screaming brat. May the Force be with you.

—*A.L.*
SAN FRANCISCO, CALIFORNIA
13M

OH, BOY!

IF YOU HAVE BOYS, CHANGE THE DIAPER FAST. And never lay a baby on an expensive Persian rug in your husband's boss's home.

> *—LISA ARMONY*
> *SHERMAN OAKS, CALIFORNIA*
> *5 2*

• • • • • • • • •

IF IT'S A BOY, USE TWO DIAPERS. Use one to cover up his business, because he is going to pee again, just as soon as you pull that wet diaper off and the cold air hits him. It's like that old camp trick where you put someone's hand in water while they are sleeping.

> *—CLIFF JOHNSON*
> *WICHITA, KANSAS*
> *50 48 45*

• • • • • • • • •

THIS IS KIND OF GROSS, but you should really avoid talking when you change a baby boy's diaper. They squirt and when that little hose goes off, you want to make sure you have your mouth closed. It only happened to me once, but it was horrible.

> *—ANGIE GUILLEN*
> *LYTLE, TEXAS*
> *23M*

NO DIAPER IS FOOLPROOF. We were guests in my cousins' house, having a nice dinner, and I had my daughter on my lap when my husband heard this small noise. He looked down at the ground, thinking the baby was dropping food from the table. Instead, she was pooping out of her diaper in a fountain onto the floor. Luckily, my cousins have a good sense of humor.

—C.S.
SAN FRANCISCO, CALIFORNIA
1

• • • • • • • •

DIAPER GENIES AREN'T WORTH THE COST or hassle. We used to use a Diaper Genie, but it was inconvenient and too complicated to use. I found it was much easier to just use a small trashcan, and keep a bunch of plastic grocery bags handy to wrap soiled diapers.

—L.O.
SYRACUSE, NEW YORK
3 1

• • • • • • • •

ONE OF THE THINGS MY HUSBAND and I found extremely helpful right away is using a hair dryer at the changing table. Not only does it provide heat and air to keep baby dry and warm (if you let them air dry you run the risk of a fountain!) but the "white noise" of a hair dryer on "low" also soothes them. As soon as our son would start to fuss, the hair dryer went on and he was instantly calmed and comforted.

—PAM IVALDI
DUBLIN, CALIFORNIA
4M

INFANT INFO

It takes approximately 500 years for a disposable diaper to break down in a landfill.

PLAY GAMES AND ENTERTAIN YOUR BABY while changing her diaper. If that doesn't work, prepare to gut it out. I sang songs. I played "This little piggy . . ." I made kissing noises. I would go through different body parts, and end by tickling her—anything to make the experience more fun.

—*L.O.*
SYRACUSE, NEW YORK
3 1

I figure that if I'm near a baby and holding a diaper bag that I automatically look cool because people love to see an involved father.

—*BRETT*
COLUMBUS, OHIO
7 4M

YOU DON'T HAVE TO CHANGE THE BABY'S DIAPER if s/he is not wet. Diapers are highly absorbent, and a little liquid is not going to mandate a full changing.

—*MELISSA STEIN*
3

IF YOU HAVE DOGS, MAKE SURE YOU CLOSE the door to the baby's room when you leave the house. Dogs like to eat dirty diapers.

—*JWAIII*
ATLANTA, GEORGIA
5 2

BUY DIAPERS A LITTLE BIT BIGGER than your baby needs—not a lot, but large enough so that they will contain the mess better.

—*ANONYMOUS*
GREENWICH, CONNECTICUT
7W

A DIAPER GENIE IS A MUST-HAVE, especially in the summer.

—*DAVE BAUDER*
CROTON-ON-HUDSON, NEW YORK
5 3

7

Moms & Dads: Read This! (Separately)

There's nothing like new parenthood to point out the differences between men and women—and we're not just talking about Anatomy 101. Moms and dads also encounter different psychological challenges in their new roles. Here are some stories and tips from the front lines of parenthood.

FOR MOMS

FIRST-TIME MOTHERHOOD IS A 24/7 learning experience, but the most important thing I can say is to trust your instincts. You won't realize how much you really know about being a mother until you're going through it, and then you'll see: Women are made to be mothers.

—*SUSAN MAROSITZ*
CLIFTON, NEW JERSEY
19M

TAKE A SHOWER BEFORE YOUR HUSBAND GOES TO WORK.

—*L.G.*
WEST NEW YORK, NEW JERSEY
2

I HAD THOUGHT A LOT ABOUT BEING PREGNANT and enjoyed all the attention during the pregnancy. But as soon as the baby was born, life changed completely. No one gave me any attention anymore; everyone focused on the baby. And my husband and I were not as flexible anymore.

—*Paget Perrault*
Melbourne, Australia
35 30

What surprised me is how the baby comes first. Always. Every time.

—*M.S.L.*
Waikoloa, Hawaii
40 37

• • • • • • • • •

THE HARDEST PART OF PREGNANCY FOR ME was when it was over. I couldn't stand looking pregnant after the fact. I handled this by working out regularly, eating right, but also enjoying the baby and not being too hard on myself. I quickly realized that you can't get back your body in a couple months, like some magazines would have you believe.

—*Vanessa Wilkinson*
Colora, Maryland
3 5M

• • • • • • • • •

MY HUSBAND IS A GREAT DAD and picks up a lot of the slack, but it's still hard. I think he wants to live in a sitcom from the '50s where after a long day he comes home to a perfect house with a perfect wife and perfect kids. That's never going to happen, but hopefully when I get more used to having both kids all the time he can at least come home to a house that's not a complete disaster, a wife that's not pulling her hair out, and two children that are wonderful, even though they're not perfect.

—*Sarah Sisson Christensen*
San Diego, California
2 2M

MY COLLEGE ROOMMATES AND I CREATED a Mommy Group over the Internet. Between all of us, we've got nearly a dozen kids ranging from babies to teens. So no matter what question you have, somebody has some relevant experience they can share with you. Plus, it keeps us all in touch.

—*K.B.*
SAN FRANCISCO, CALIFORNIA
6 3 3M

Don't judge your husband too harshly.

—*ANONYMOUS*
LIVERPOOL, NEW YORK
7 5

> "When you have your first baby, it is a monumental change in life. You go through a period of mourning/grief for the old life that is lost, and never to be known again. Life will never be the same as it was before."

—*SHER JOHNSON*
EL SEGUNDO, CALIFORNIA
11 8 5.5M

I FEEL LIKE I TOOK A HUGE STEP in being a woman when I had a baby. When other mothers looked at me, it was like they were saying, "Welcome to the club!" I feel a strong connection to my mother as well as other mothers because of it.

—*LESLIE BUNDY*
WAUKESHA, WISCONSIN
1

IN YOUR DREAMS

There's nothing more exciting than being pregnant for the first time. You can visualize exactly how it will be—your angelic little baby smiling up at you, happily breast-feeding. You know the rules you'll set—no videos, no pacifier, no artificial colors or flavors, maybe you'll even cultivate a garden and only feed your baby foods that come from your own pesticide-free soil. Yet here you are, six months later, in line at Target buying Gerber's turkey-ham surprise and Barney videos, while your baby is propped in the stroller happily alternating between its pacifier and bottle.

Don't let others define for you what makes a "perfect" mom. A "perfect" mom listens and responds to the needs of both her child and herself. A perfect mom is the mom who allows a pacifier if that's what will soothe the baby; who pops open the jar of Gerber's or can of formula if that's what will make it easier and therefore less stressful for her; who sets up the playpen in front of a video for five minutes so she can take a shower.

—Andrea Menschel
Calabasas, California
8 5

MY HUSBAND IS SUCH A COMPETENT, confident person that not knowing exactly what to do with our baby was unfamiliar territory for him. After quite a few arguments, I realized that it's critical to make a father feel competent. Encourage and support him with his baby and give him lots of opportunities to succeed. For example, in the beginning let him hold the baby at times when the baby's likely to be calm.

—*ROBYN*
BIGLERVILLE, PENNSYLVANIA
1

After spending the day giving everything I have to the baby, I hate to say it, but there isn't a lot left for me to give to my husband.

—*M.C.*
FAIRFAX, CALIFORNIA
11W

YOU MAY NOT BOND IMMEDIATELY with your new baby. Sometimes it takes a while to get used to being a mom. Don't feel you're inept or undeserving just because you're not instantly enamored with this little wrinkled, crying, pee-and-poop machine!

—*ANONYMOUS*
ALAMEDA, CALIFORNIA
7M

HERE'S A PIECE OF ADVICE that many mothers receive, but few follow: Take time for yourself. Babies are sweet, cute, cuddly, and very demanding. All the time. As they grow into toddlers, they are still sweet, cute, cuddly, and even more demanding. All the time. When I say to take time for yourself, I mean to go away for at least one week every year. Go someplace where you can relax and take care of yourself. Don't feel guilty. Leave the child with your husband and/or parents. They'll be fine. And you'll be even better when you return. (Start planning next year's trip shortly after you return!)

—*E.G.*
NEW HAVEN, CONNECTICUT
20

DON'T BE FOOLED BY ALL THE PEOPLE who paint parenthood as this rosy, soft-focus thing. It's hard every single day. There are days during the first few weeks of parenthood where the baby does nothing but cry and eat and poop, and you'll be tired and cranky and you'll wish you had never gotten pregnant. And that's OK. You aren't evil if you sometimes regret this huge thing that happened. Those thoughts are usually fleeting. And it does get better and easier over time.

—R.
REDMOND, WASHINGTON
6

> No matter what you do, your pre-baby life is never coming back.

—MARGARET KEENE
HERMOSA BEACH, CALIFORNIA
8M

Whatever you do, never, EVER allow your husband to dress the baby.

—NICOLE LESSIN
HELOTES, TEXAS
17M

I'M IN A DINNER CLUB WITH A GROUP of women. We run the gamut—professional women, a 39-year-old friend who was recently engaged, a few moms who work, some who don't. There's a sense that we all want to be able to quote the front page of the Wall Street Journal, prepare a gourmet dinner for our family after a day in court, plan our child's birthday party, and watch their gymnastics class . . . but you can't do it all.

—MARYBETH
SAN FRANCISCO, CALIFORNIA
4

BABY BLUES

DEVELOP POSTPARTUM RITUALS. Every day for a month after I gave birth to twins I broke down in tears at four p.m. At first it wore us out. Then, one day, my husband noticed I was about to hit that low and he said, "Are you about to have high tea?" After that, every day when I felt "high tea" coming on he sat me down in the same living room chair and brought me a beer and a box of Kleenex. I cried, sipped my beer, and sat. Knowing we had developed this ritual together made my "high tea" something that I did not dread or fear.

—*S.*
PORTLAND, MAINE
-5 1

• • • • • • • •

POSTPARTUM DEPRESSION IS BY FAR THE MOST IMPORTANT ISSUE that most people are reluctant to discuss. Before I gave birth, I thought it only happened to people who didn't want kids, had an unplanned pregnancy, were single parents or had a bad relationship with their partners. None of these applied to me. But within days of giving birth, I experienced such extreme PPD that I was beside myself. I was convinced that I'd made a horrible mistake in having the baby and wished someone else would take her! Fortunately, I had a very understanding gynecologist who diagnosed me and gave me some very fast-acting antidepressants. Within a week I was stabilized and after three months I began to bond and love my baby.

—*ANONYMOUS*
ALAMEDA, CALIFORNIA
7M

• • • • • • • •

FOR THE "BABY BLUES," GO TO ACUPUNCTURE—it gets everything aligned. Acupuncture in general helps to relax and balance energy, which often is enough to ease depression.

—*MARIANNE*
SAN FRANCISCO, CALIFORNIA
4 5M

Before the baby, I was very much into working long hours, making money, shopping, working out and making sure I looked good. Now that the baby is here, I still have over 20 pounds gained from the pregnancy after seven months, but I would prefer to stay with my daughter than to go to the gym and work out.

—*Maria Ferranti*
Toronto, Ontario, Canada
7M

"Never say, 'My child will never have a crusty nose,' or, 'I would never take my child out with a cough.'"

—*Kelli Scharff*
Springfield, Illinois
19 17

I experience so much stress and worry all the time. I'm able to manage it by talking to my husband and remembering the good times.

—*Beth*
Oklahoma
6

We were still living in my husband's "bachelor pad" when the baby was born. It was hot, and, with our new addition, crowded. My husband called from work to say he was going to be 15 minutes late. When he walked in the door, I flipped out. I needed that time—even if it was only 15 minutes—for myself. My husband saw and smelled how everything was—the milk, the spit-up, the diapers, the heat—he said, "This used to be my Shangri-La." Having lost my 15 minutes of "alone time" and with hormones on the fritz, I responded, "This is my jail!"

—*Marybeth*
San Francisco, California
4

REMEMBER S-E-X?

SEX AFTER BABY—WHAT A MILESTONE. The first time is an interesting experience, for sure. But it slowly gets back to what it was like before baby.

—*ADRIANE*
FT. LAUDERDALE, FLORIDA
1

• • • • • • • •

SEX WHILE BREASTFEEDING CAN BE SURPRISING. The first time we did it, we had warm, sticky milk all over us. It was quite a shock. We learned after that to let the kid eat, then make love.

—*V.B.*
DOHA, QATAR
23 21 14

• • • • • • • •

TONS OF PEOPLE WILL TELL YOU THAT IT'S IMPOSSIBLE, or difficult, to get pregnant while breastfeeding. Don't count on it. My mother got pregnant while still nursing a three-month old, and I got pregnant while nursing a seven-month old. Lucky for us, we both wanted those second babies, because the nursing certainly didn't prevent them from coming!

—*SHANNON L.*
SAN RAFAEL, CALIFORNIA
16 15 13

• • • • • • • •

WHEN THE DOCTORS SAY SIX WEEKS until you can start having sex again, they should really say two years. Then you'd feel good about the three times you did it last year!

—*SHAUNA*
VANCOUVER, BC, CANADA
2 8M

PEOPLE SAID, "IT'S GOING TO CHANGE YOUR LIFE," but no one prepared us for the massive emotional and social shift in our lives. You've got to change your whole way of being; suddenly you're focused on this one little individual and you're much less focused on each other.

—*NANCY*
PORTLAND, MAINE
2

I THINK IT TAKES TIME AND PATIENCE for a woman to find her "mommy identity" and make peace with herself—with the body she is left with after a baby has been through it, with the lack of freedom, with the new responsibilities, with the change in your marriage relationship, and the changing roles as you become parents.

—*SHER JOHNSON*
EL SEGUNDO, CALIFORNIA
11 8 5.5M

INFANT INFO

There are more than twice as many 40-something moms now as there were 20 years ago.

FACT: RETAILERS STRATEGICALLY PLACE diapers near beer knowing full well that a man's quick run to the store for diapers can result in added purchases. Therefore, make sure you leave the man at home with the baby and you make the diaper run!

—*MARTHA*
SPRINGFIELD, ILLINOIS
17 12 7

TRY NOT TO GET JEALOUS IF YOUR MATE has better luck quieting down the baby, or if it seems like your newborn likes him more than you. Things have a way of shifting, and besides—you are in this together, for the long run, so try not to get petty.

—*MOLLY F.*
NEW YORK, NEW YORK

Having kids close in age is more difficult than having twins. At least twins are going through the same stages together and wearing the same size clothes and diapers! My girls are 15 months apart, and are always in slightly different stages.

—*Donna*
Allentown, Pennsylvania
7 6

Don't take the baby shopping or you will never buy anything for yourself again. Ask your husband to buy you a gift certificate to a boutique that sells women's clothing only and not cute little baby summer dresses.

—*Janie Scott*
San Antonio, Texas
5M

Before the baby, my husband and I used to walk to the local Dairy Queen some evenings for a sundae. One day after my baby was born, we were taking our walk and realized that we had forgotten all about our one-week old son: He was still at home by himself! That's when I realized that everything was different.

—*Paget Perrault*
Melbourne, Australia
35 30

There's nothing like a long day at the office to make a man realize how much he misses his baby.

—*Armin Brott*
Oakland, California
13 10 7M

FOR DADS

After your wife has a baby, be home with her more. Wake up in the middle of the night and help. Some men run away. But I think you need to share. It's not just her child; it's yours, too.

—*Batia Elkayam*
Los Angeles, California

I'M THE ORGANIZER OF A DAD'S GROUP, and people are always asking me if I think there's a difference between dads and moms. In over six years of intensive interaction with full-time moms and full-time dads, I have determined that there is very little difference between the moms and dads, except that—on average—the dads drink significantly more beer.

—*EVAN WEISSMAN*
OAKLAND, CALIFORNIA
6 3

One of the most surprising things to me as a new parent was the sheer amount of love I had for my new daughter. I never knew I could love anything so much.

—*WAYNE DRASH*
ATLANTA, GEORGIA
2

DON'T LET YOUR WIFE SUFFER through the nights alone. Participate. The woman gets the worst of it, particularly if she is going to breastfeed because there's nothing you can do to help with that. So I got up in the middle of the night when we were giving bottles, changed diapers, etc.

—*FRANK TRASK*
CHARLESTON, SOUTH CAROLINA
36 34 31 26

WHEN YOU HAVE AN OPPORTUNITY TO BE WITH your child, be there 100 percent. Forget the phone, forget the newspaper, forget the TV, forget washing the dishes, and forget eating if you can. You can do all those things after the baby goes to sleep.

—*ARMIN BROTT*
OAKLAND, CALIFORNIA
13 10 7M

IF YOU ARE BOTTLE-FEEDING, I suggest dads feed the baby at least once a day. That will help them bond, as well as help mom.

—*SHARI LEE SUGARMAN*
NORTH BABYLON, NEW YORK
9W

GET IT WHILE YOU CAN

HOW DO MEN TURN OFF THAT NEED FOR SEX in those weeks after childbirth? Honestly, we can't. We're men, aren't we? But know that it will be a while before you get into that promised land. So, wait on your wife hand and foot. Give her everything she needs. Then during that hour the baby is asleep, ask her to service you. A hand job is a wonderful thing when you haven't had sex for a month.

—*ANONYMOUS*
SYRACUSE, NEW YORK
8 4 17M 5D

I ALWAYS GET UP AT NIGHT because I am breastfeeding, so my husband lets me sleep in one weekend morning. Just knowing I can sleep in makes me feel less tired. He also does a little more tidying up around the house in the evening so that we both get some time to relax.

—*SHAUNA FARRELL*
VANCOUVER, BC, CANADA
2 8M

FATHERS GENERALLY TAKE TWO WEEKS of paternity leave after the birth. The problem is there isn't a tremendous amount a dad can do directly related to the baby. The mother is nursing nonstop and that's all the baby sees or wants. So my husband took his two weeks off and built a deck on the house. He felt it was the best, most productive use of his time, and it was the best expression of love possible.

—*MARIANNE*
SAN FRANCISCO, CALIFORNIA
4 5M

BABY'S FAVORITE

I RECOMMEND THAT ALL DADS TAKE CARE of their kids, alone, for a large chunk of time: a whole day, a weekend—and not just once, but regularly. It gives them a chance to learn how to relate to the baby in their own unique way.

—*JOHN KIM*
LOS ANGELES, CALIFORNIA
2

• • • • • • • •

FEED YOUR BABIES, CHANGE THEM, PLAY WITH THEM, take them for car rides, whatever puts the two of you together. When you walk in the house at the end of the day and hear "Dad-eeeeeeeee!" and a pair of little feet running to the door, it's an amazing feeling.

—*LT. COL. DAVE EATON, USAF*
FT. WALTON BEACH, FLORIDA
12 11

• • • • • • • •

DAD SHOULD BE LEFT ALONE WITH THE BABY, so he can't pass him or her off to his mom or someone else. Often, it is their insecurity about the baby that makes them hesitant to help with the baby care. Once they know they can do it, both you and he can relax.

—*SHARI LEE SUGARMAN*
NORTH BABYLON, NEW YORK
9W

• • • • • • • •

LET YOUR BABY HEAR YOUR HEART. I used to lay our twins on my chest so they could listen to my heartbeat and fall asleep. I read somewhere that babies can get to know you this way.

—*PAT BOEA*
SYRACUSE, NEW YORK
19 17 15 12

DEVELOP A PRIVATE RITUAL WITH YOUR CHILD—something the two of you share that nobody else (including your spouse) does. When my daughter is done bathing, I wrap her up tightly in blankets and hold her close to me. It might sound simple, but moments such as these are crucial, because they're the foundation to build a lifetime of good memories upon.

—ANONYMOUS
CASTLE ROCK, COLORADO
3

• • • • • • • •

ANYTHING PHYSICAL—TOSSING BABY IN THE AIR, swinging them, raspberries on tummy, severe tickling—will help you bond with your baby. Mom may not like it but baby sure will.

—MARK KAPLAN
FOSTER CITY, CALIFORNIA
3 1

• • • • • • • •

DADS, BE GOOFY! Funny faces, funny voices, dancing, singing—I do it all.

—DAN DUPONT
ARLINGTON, VIRGINIA
6 3 3M

ONE NIGHT MY FRIEND STEVE was over. I was holding my son, and he threw up all over me. My wife yelled, "Quick, get a rag!" So Steve ran to the kitchen, got a rag, and started cleaning me off. Then my wife yelled, "No, not him—the rug!" That gave me a pretty good sense of my status.

—JOEL ROSENFELD
NEW YORK, NEW YORK
-17 15

"Don't underestimate how much energy it takes your wife to care for a newborn."

—ANONYMOUS
LIVERPOOL, NEW YORK
7 5

HUSBANDS, HELP YOUR WIVES WITH THE NIGHT feedings. If your wife is breastfeeding, walk over to the nursery and bring the baby to her to nurse, and then carry the baby back to the nursery. Not only will this provide some much-needed relief for your wife, it will reinforce the feeling that you are a team.

—JAN
ALLENTOWN, PENNSYLVANIA
3 2

I'VE FOUND THAT A LOT OF BABIES ARE COMFORTED by what my wife calls my "daddy magic." I just cradle the baby with my hand behind the child's head, my forearm beneath their back (so the baby's legs are on either side of my upper arm) and either rock them or pat/rub them gently with my left hand. There have been a number of social occasions where I've been called in from another room to rock an unhappy infant down for his/her nap.

—*Jay Johnson*
Lansing, Michigan
13 11 8 20M

MY HUSBAND'S A VERY ORGANIZED GUY and, immediately after our daughter's birth, he didn't have any project to get accomplished. To stay busy he created an Excel spreadsheet of the baby's schedule—when she fed (and on which breast), when she pooped, when she slept. It was a great system. And when you speak to a pediatrician who asks when the last time your baby fed/pooped/slept, having readily available data is key.

—*Marybeth*
San Francisco, California
4

WHEN YOU COME HOME don't ask your wife, "What did you do today?" It sounds like you think she didn't do anything. Instead ask her, "How was your day?" And listen when she responds, even if it's all complaints.

—*Lee Montopoli*
River Dale, New Jersey
3 5M

INFANT INFO

If you thought it was coincidence that a baby begins to stir when mommy walks into the room, think again. Newborns can recognize the smell of their mothers' breastmilk.

My husband helps me by letting me have time to myself and taking care of the girls when I need a break.

—*Cassie DeMille*
Fairchild AFB, Washington
2 2M

Babies seem to realize there's a difference between how Mommy and Daddy do things, and they accept both ways. My wife can make my baby giggle by kissing her all over, but she rarely laughs like that for me. I make her laugh by flying her through the air, but she almost never laughs when my wife does the same thing.

—*John Kim*
Los Angeles, California
2

• • • • • • • • •

The first kid changes your whole outlook on life. Being a father changes your responsibility to your family. I suddenly had a realization about my career, and I had to take a step back and consider where I was going, how to get serious and make real money.

—*Chuck S.*
Ponte Vedra Beach, Florida
9 4

8 Sleep? The ABCs of ZZZs

Do you find yourself daydreaming about sleep? Do you envy your child-less friends who casually mention sleeping "way too late" on the weekends? Are you having trouble reading this? Grab a cup of coffee. You're not alone. For tips on how to get your baby to sleep, and how you can sneak in some shut-eye, you just have to keep your eyes open long enough to get through this chapter.

JUST GIVE UP THE NOTION THAT YOU WILL have a full night's sleep for years. It makes life easier—albeit more fatiguing.

—*DICKIE*
ATLANTA, GEORGIA
6M

WHEN THE BABY CRIES IN THE MIDDLE OF THE NIGHT, DON'T ARGUE ABOUT GETTING UP. JUST BE GLAD YOU GET TO DO IT!

—*MARK*
NEW YORK, NEW YORK

I GET ABOUT SIX HOURS A NIGHT (not all at one time). My daughter wakes up every two to two and half hours. On my husband's days off, I sleep all day. This really helps me get through the week. Before my baby was born, I slept 10 to 12 hours a night (no kidding!!) so this was a huge change!

—SARAH CROMWELL
RIVERBANK, CALIFORNIA
3M

• • • • • • • •

ALWAYS GET UP BEFORE YOUR CHILD WAKES, whether to read the paper and have coffee, do yoga, meditate. If you don't have some alone time in the morning, your day is spent playing catch-up. As soon as I hear a bird chirp, I think, "Grab this moment!"

—P. SUPPIGER
OAKLAND, CALIFORNIA
5 2

• • • • • • • •

WITH MY DAUGHTER, I LENGTHENED THE AMOUNT of time she slept at a stretch. During the day, I kept her awake longer and longer after nursing by playing with her and distracting her. Slowly she adjusted and slept for longer periods at night, too. By eight weeks, she slept through the night. I was so grateful!

—CHRISTY
ALLENTOWN, PENNSYLVANIA
4 2

• • • • • • • •

I WISH I'D KNOWN THE EXTENT OF SLEEP deprivation that motherhood brings. My babies didn't sleep through the night until they stopped nursing, so I literally don't think I got a real night's sleep for three years or so.

—RACHEL LEON
CROTON-ON-HUDSON, NEW YORK
5 3

My mom told me to sleep when the baby sleeps, and clean when he's awake. I took her advice, and was only half the zombie I would have been otherwise.

—A.B.
27 -23
21 10

WHEN MY KIDS WERE BABIES, I had my fair share of nights when they didn't want to go to sleep. Instead of driving them around in the car like most people do, I found it easier to take them for walks in their strollers. I think it was a combination of the cool evening air and the motion of the stroller, but they'd usually be asleep before we'd walked a couple of blocks.

—*HELEN REICH*
DUBOIS, PENNSYLVANIA
43 38 33

"I just wish there was a way to stock up on sleep, create a reserve and use it after the baby comes."

—*ADRIANE*
FT. LAUDERDALE, FLORIDA
1

MY OLDEST BOY DID NOT SLEEP for the first six months of his life unless he was on a warm body or somehow moving. In fact, for many weeks the only place he would sleep for more that an hour or so was a swing. I still vividly remember the panic surging through me when the batteries started to die in the middle of the night.

—*EMILY*
FREEPORT, MAINE
7 6

What's the secret to getting the kid back to sleep? I have no idea, since I can't really remember the first three months of his life.

—*DAVE COHEN*

SWING SHIFT

For the first couple months of my daughter's life, my wife and I followed a two nights on/two nights off parenting rotation, which was a lifesaver! One of us assumed complete responsibility for the baby's middle-of-the-night needs (changing, feeding, etc.), while the other slept in the guest room with a pillow over his/her head, and concentrated exclusively on getting a good night's sleep. It prevented burnout—48 hours is plenty of time to rejuvenate, and just enough to exhaust the other person.

—Jordan Graham
Parker, Colorado
8 1

• • • • • • • •

With our twins, each of us would take one child for a whole day. We would each feed, change, bathe, and wake up in the middle of the night for the child under our supervision for a full 24 hours. Then we would switch. This way, we could bond with each child and also keep track of diaper changes and feedings. And after our daughter started sleeping through the night at three months, we were each guaranteed a good night's rest every other night.

—M.A.
Connecticut
-3

• • • • • • • •

Take turns doing the midnight feedings so that each parent gets at least a night or two per week of nearly-full sleep. I worked outside the house, so my wife let me sleep during the week. In exchange I always took Friday and Saturday night. Not only did it help the wife and kids, I think it helped our marriage!

—M.S.
New York, New York
18 13

I THINK A BABY SHOULD BE IN A BEDTIME routine where at a certain hour every night we put her to sleep. Even if the baby cries when you do it, you have to just put the baby down and go to sleep yourselves at some point.

—JOE AGUILAR
MANDELEIN, ILLINOIS
13M

> "When it comes to getting a baby to sleep, what works for one won't necessarily work for another. You have to adapt."

—CHRISTINE MCCARTHY
PORT-ZELIENOPLE, PENNSYLVANIA
6 4 3 1.5

OUR BABY SLEPT THROUGH THE NIGHT after only three weeks! We made sure to only swaddle her at night and not have her take naps in her nighttime sleep area (crib) so that she knew the difference between night and day. She napped in the living room during the day.

—ANONYMOUS
ALAMEDA, CALIFORNIA
7M

INFANT INFO

Infants average almost 90 minutes less sleep a day than the 14-hour minimum doctors recommend.

TALK WITH YOUR SPOUSE about your middle-of-the-night plan before you go to sleep and even write down your promises. It's really hard in the middle of the night—when you're delirious and frustrated—to remember and stick to a plan. It helped us support each other when the baby screamed and cried.

—*ANNE B.*
SAN FRANCISCO, CALIFORNIA
1

"If you don't sleep when the baby's sleeping, you're sunk. Take naps."

—*SHIRLEY GUTKOWSKI*
SUN PRAIRIE, WISCONSIN
26 25 -23 21

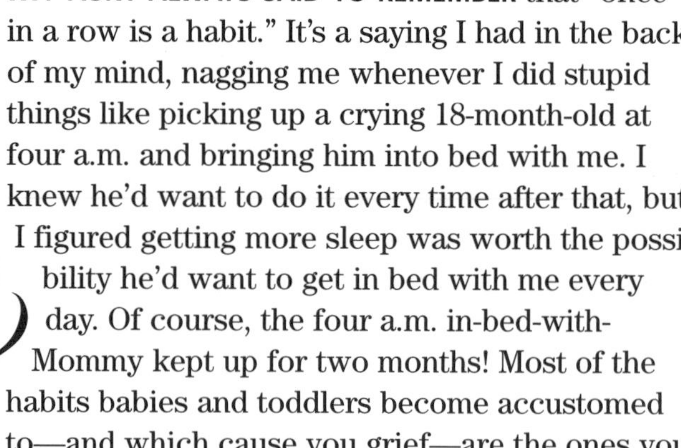

MY AUNT ALWAYS SAID TO REMEMBER that "once in a row is a habit." It's a saying I had in the back of my mind, nagging me whenever I did stupid things like picking up a crying 18-month-old at four a.m. and bringing him into bed with me. I knew he'd want to do it every time after that, but I figured getting more sleep was worth the possibility he'd want to get in bed with me every day. Of course, the four a.m. in-bed-with-Mommy kept up for two months! Most of the habits babies and toddlers become accustomed to—and which cause you grief—are the ones you create for them.

—*CHRISTINE BEIDEL*
RUTHERFORD, NEW JERSEY
11 2

IT SOOTHES THE SOUL

DEVELOP A NAP-TIME ROUTINE. I read my kids a book, then they listen to music. That's how they fall asleep. We play stuff like Chicago and Neil Diamond for them through their entire nap-time. It works.

—*FORREST*
WELLINGTON, COLORADO
3 2

• • • • • • • •

CALMING CDS THAT BABIES AND GROWNUPS LOVE:

Waltz for Debby, Bill Evans
Kind of Blue, Miles Davis
Door Harp, Michael Houser
Solo Monk, Thelonius Monk

—*KENNY F.*
RED BOILING SPRINGS, TENNESSEE
3

• • • • • • • •

MUSIC WAS ONE OF THE KEY ELEMENTS to getting our baby to sleep. Soothing tunes were ones that contain no vocals—which seem to be distracting. For infants, try ones that also contain heartbeat sounds. My daughter, now four years old, still conks out when she listens to her favorite ragtime CD at bedtime.

—*C. KARP*
IRVINE, CALIFORNIA
4

• • • • • • • •

IF YOU GET THEM ADDICTED TO SLEEPING with white noise tapes or music, that's the only way they'll be able to sleep. We made that mistake on our first baby. For our second kid, we just forced him to learn to fall asleep in silence, and once he got the hang of it, he was a much better sleeper than our daughter.

—*M.S.*
NEW YORK, NEW YORK
18 13

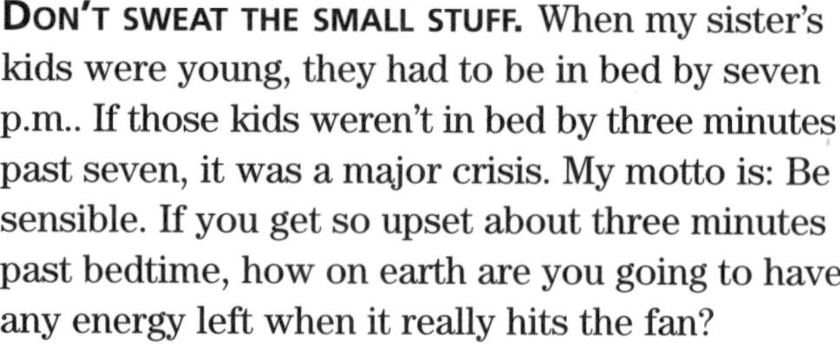

DON'T SWEAT THE SMALL STUFF. When my sister's kids were young, they had to be in bed by seven p.m.. If those kids weren't in bed by three minutes past seven, it was a major crisis. My motto is: Be sensible. If you get so upset about three minutes past bedtime, how on earth are you going to have any energy left when it really hits the fan?

—*JERENE*
WILLIAMSPORT, PENNSYLVANIA
13 12 -7

The key is to marry someone who functions best when you don't. If you're both tired, you're going to kill each other. If you get rest, you'll survive.

—*D.M.*
IOWA CITY, IOWA
16 13

DON'T PUT THE BABY IN YOUR BED. The baby will get used to the warmth, the body contact. Get them used to sleeping in their own bed. We had a bassinet for our daughter right next to our bed. It kept her more comfortable, and she didn't wake up as much. It also helped us get sleep. If we heard a grunt, it was just a matter of looking over the bed rather than getting up.

—*J.B.*
EAST SYRACUSE, NEW YORK
2

SLEEP TRAINING FALLS INTO TWO CAMPS: the CIO (cry it out) crowd and the AP (attachment parenting) crowd. Most parents I talked to said that CIO was the only thing that worked. Some struggled for years until they tried it. I thought for sure I was going to be AP, but after six months I had an experience that made me change my mind. He was crying in his crib, really wailing, and my husband and I rushed in and picked him up to see what was wrong. He immediately stopped crying and started smiling and laughing. That's when I knew I'd been had. I decided we should start sleep training and put him on a pretty strict sleeping schedule. It worked like a charm.

—*BARBARA MCGLAMERY*

THE BEST OF A BAD SITUATION

When our first was born, he used to cry those first few months because he was restless and couldn't sleep. Because my wife had the baby for the entire day, nighttime duties—including feedings—were my responsibility. I used to go into his room and just walk with him on my shoulder and hum, and while he would never fully sleep, he would calm down. Sometimes he would hum, too. The trick was that I knew this would be our routine every night, so I planned on it and looked forward to it, and I didn't try to rush back to bed.

Even though I got little sleep those first months, I found myself looking forward to the evening time I spent with my son. I told myself that no matter how much I wanted to be in bed, this was actually more enjoyable because it doesn't last, since they grow up so quickly. I was right. He's 14 now, and it seems like only yesterday he was a baby. I think of those evenings as fondly now as I felt when I was going through it.

—Tim O'Brien
Pittsburgh, Pennsylvania
14

THE FATHER'S UNABRIDGED GUIDE TO AVOIDING CHILD CARE

New fathers will be shocked to learn that, even though they haven't been outfitted with mammaries, they will be fully expected to participate in the raising of an infant. Particularly horrifying is when the baby starts crying in the middle of the night, and the father is expected to get up and change diapers.

To get out of this duty, follow what I call the "W. Bruce Cameron Dictionary Method." Buy a thick hardcover dictionary of the English language, wrap it in towels, and place it in the baby's bedroom.

The next time the baby starts crying in the middle of the night, whisper sweetly to your wife, "Don't worry, honey, I'll take care of it." When you get to the baby's room, lift the dictionary above your head and drop it straight to the floor. This will make a loud bang that will resonate throughout every room of the house. Immediately afterward, scoop up your baby into your arms, and when your wife comes rushing in with a panicked look on her face, crying, "What just happened?" you can look back at her innocently and reply, "What do you mean? I didn't hear anything."

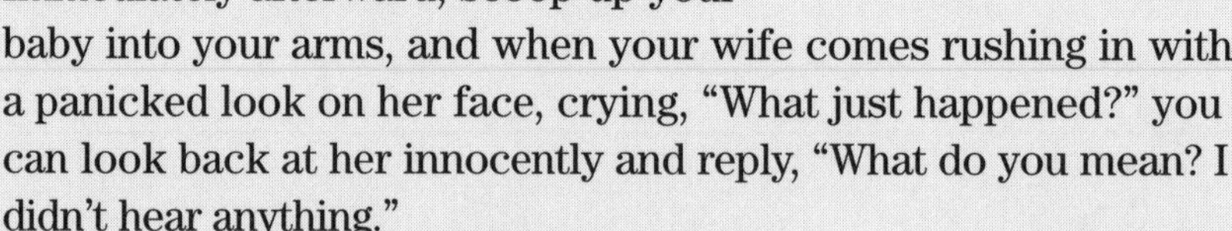

From this point forward, every time the baby cries in the middle of the night, she will insist on getting up to take care of it herself.

—*W. Bruce Cameron*
Santa Monica, California
22 20 16

BABIES DO NOT BELONG IN THEIR PARENTS' BED under any circumstances. Even if you're not having sex, your bed has a feeling of intimacy associated with it, and adding a child to the equation ruins it.

—*STEVEN GREEN*
LOS ANGELES, CALIFORNIA
35 30 29 25 17

• • • • • • • •

IF YOU WAIT UNTIL YOUR BABY IS REALLY TIRED, he is actually overtired and will have a harder time falling asleep. Try to notice how your baby behaves right before he gets really tired and put him to sleep then, and he'll sleep better and longer.

—*K. JONES*
PHILADELPHIA, PENNSYLVANIA
14 10 6

• • • • • • • •

FIGURE OUT WHAT WORKS FOR YOUR CHILD—and know that everyone is different. The only thing that worked to put my daughter to sleep was putting her in a sturdy backpack and walking around, until she fell asleep. For a time, it was the ONLY thing she'd sleep in.

—*TINA SMITH*
FORT COLLINS, COLORADO
4 2

• • • • • • • •

YOU WILL FIND YOURSELF PROMISING your new child just about anything in the world if they will just go back to sleep after their middle-of-the-night feeding. By the middle of the second month, if my kid had been able to tally all the promises, I'd be out a fleet of new BMW's when he turns 16, a few motorcycles, a couple of all-expense-paid trips to Europe and Australia, and season passes to Disneyland every year.

—*DAVE COHEN*

Put the bassinet in the living room with you while you're watching TV. It teaches the baby to sleep through a lot of noise.

—*ANONYMOUS*
WASHINGTON, DC
12

It's never too early to start a bedtime routine. It will help them go to sleep better right away, and especially down the road.

—A.L.
Boston, Massachusetts
6 4

DON'T LET YOUR BABY SLEEP WITH YOU, unless you really want to. We made the mistake of letting him sleep with us in the beginning. So at six months, we had to break him of the habit, which was hard. Luckily it only took a day or two, with a couple of hours of crying each night.

—Bethany
Fort Collins, Colorado
11M

• • • • • • • •

A LOT OF PEOPLE SAY NOT TO LET YOUR KIDS SLEEP in your bed, but I don't agree with that. We let our children sleep with us until they were two to three years old and it has made them more confident.

—Anna Edelman
Brooklyn, New York
7 2 7M

• • • • • • • •

THE WHOLE FAMILY IS BETTER OFF if you get some sleep. Sleep deprivation makes you act out of character. I would lose my temper. I would forget things. When my baby was six weeks old, I would hear him wake up, and I would just start crying.

—L.
Charlotte, North Carolina
2 1

• • • • • • • •

ONCE I ACCEPTED THAT IT WOULD BE a very long time before I would sleep through the night, it made it much easier.

—Suzanne Nayduch
Fort Collins, Colorado
8M

9

Crying: It Can Drive You to Tears

There's nothing more nervewracking than trying to calm a screaming baby who can't tell you what's wrong, and doesn't understand a soothing word you're saying anyway. Take heart—there are ways to get your baby to relax. And ways to help you *relax, too. Read on to find an answer to your cry for help . . .*

A BABY CAN SENSE WHEN YOU'RE STRESSED. You have to stay calm, even if your heart is in your throat. Try to soothe instead of getting involved in the hysteria your baby is involved in. The more stressed you get, the more it rubs off on your baby.

—*J.B.H.*
ALEXANDRIA, VIRGINIA
3M

ONE WORD: EARPLUGS.

—*JOHN RODGERS*
SEATTLE, WASHINGTON
9

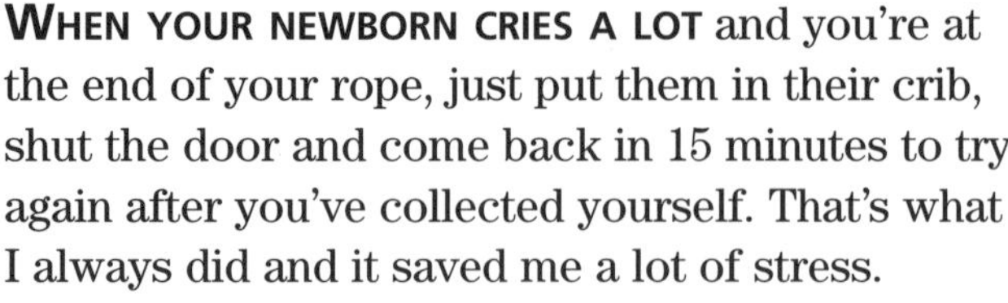

WHEN YOUR NEWBORN CRIES A LOT and you're at the end of your rope, just put them in their crib, shut the door and come back in 15 minutes to try again after you've collected yourself. That's what I always did and it saved me a lot of stress.

—*KRISTI*
CEDAR RAPIDS, IOWA
2

MY DAUGHTER SCREAMED FOR THE ENTIRE first year. I just tried to keep from jumping out the window. I held her incessantly and breastfed her incessantly and tried to pay attention to her as much as possible. That first year was very tough—she was not a cute baby. She was not fun.

—*DEB S.*
EL CAJON, CALIFORNIA
22 13

Remember, this, too, will pass. Remind yourself that things are not always going to be this way.

—*W.F.*
MERTZTOWN, PENNSYLVANIA
24 20

IF THE BABY IS GOING CRAZY CRYING, step out of the room, take some deep breaths, and then come back. You need to get yourself together, no matter what's happening with the child.

—*SHANI WERHLE*
ISRAEL

WHEN IT COMES TO GETTING BABIES TO STOP crying you really have to be creative. When my daughter would cry and cry for no reason, we found that giving her an ice cube to play with and suck on a little really calmed her. Bizarre but true.

—*ROB MARINO*
EAST LIVERPOOL, OHIO
19 14

THE WORST MOMENTS ARE WHEN my daughter seems to be inconsolable and I can't figure out why—she's been fed, she's clean and she's not tired. When the baby gets like that, it stresses out my wife and then I've got to deal with both of them.

—*JOHN D. CALLEY*
ALEXANDRIA, VIRGINIA
4M

"Babies don't die from crying. But they do learn from it. If you jump to respond to crying, they'll expect you to come running every time they do it."

—*CATHY*
ST. LOUIS PARK, MINNESOTA
11 *7*

MY DAUGHTER'S FIRST FEW WEEKS AT HOME, she would cry all the time. If it got unbearable, I would have to let my husband take over, or walk away for a few minutes. A screaming baby really does take its toll on the nerves.

—*MARIA FERRANTI*
TORONTO, ONTARIO, CANADA
7M

MELTDOWN IN AISLE 9

WHEN YOUR BABY IS CRYING IN LINE AT THE SUPERMARKET, distract him or her with a magazine. My son has an eye for the pretty ladies, so I usually give him Mademoiselle or some other colorful magazine to look at. That usually works.

—*A.V.*
NEW YORK, NEW YORK
18M

• • • • • • • •

KEYS AND TIC-TACS ARE GOOD DEVICES FOR SOOTHING a crying baby in the supermarket. They're like little rattles. And if your baby is old enough, sit them up on the counter or the little shelf where you sign your credit card receipts—it usually surprises them so much they stop crying.

—*DAN DUPONT*
ARLINGTON, VIRGINIA
6 3 3M

• • • • • • • •

KEEP THEM MOVING AND THEY'RE usually fine. Pick them up and rock them—it's easy enough to push the cart with your stomach if you're already in line. Or leave enough space between you and the person in front of you to rock the cart back and forth.

—*JAY JOHNSON*
LANSING, MICHIGAN
13 11 8 20M

• • • • • • • •

IF YOUR BABY IS CRYING ON LINE AT THE SUPERMARKET, look for someone who loves kids to distract him.

—*STEVEN SHELTON*
WICHITA FALLS, TEXAS
30 22

WHEN YOUR BABY CRIES, rather than getting frustrated, join the chorus. Sometimes Junior really appreciates the crooning company.

—*DICKIE*
ATLANTA, GEORGIA
6M

"A calm temperament helps, but if you don't have one you're not going to suddenly develop one when your baby is crying."

—*BARBARA STEWART*
SEATTLE, WASHINGTON
20 17

MY HUSBAND LIKES TO WAIT A LITTLE LONGER than I do to go in and check on our daughter and by then she's reaching an hysterical peak. Once I couldn't take it anymore and I went in to check on her before he was ready. She had the most fearful look in her eye—it really made me question the road we're taking with our baby. Babies are so helpless, you don't know if you're doing the right thing or not.

—*J.B.H.*
ALEXANDRIA, VIRGINIA
3M

THE GREAT PACIFIER DEBATE

DON'T USE PACIFIERS. First off, a little crying never hurt a child. Second, pacifiers are not good for the gums and teeth.

—JEANNE ECKMAN
LANCASTER, PENNSYLVANIA
11 - 5

• • • • • • • •

YOU ARE NOT "PLUGGING UP THE BABY" BY USING A PACIFIER. The ones made today are shaped so that they don't cause dental problems.

—KATHY PENTON
SAVANNAH, GEORGIA
23

• • • • • • • •

WE DIDN'T WANT TO USE A PACIFIER, but it only took one week of crying for us to give in. From the minute we put it in, he was happy. I prefer the pacifier over the thumb—we can always take the pacifier away.

—KRISTIN KELLEY
ANNANDALE, VIRGINIA
2

• • • • • • • •

IT WAS COMICAL THAT A LITTLE PIECE OF PLASTIC AND RUBBER controlled not only my daughter but me, too. One time, I took the kids sightseeing to an old military fort. When it was time to leave, the kids were tired and my daughter started crying. I tore that van apart but no pacifier! I couldn't face a 30-minute drive with her screaming the whole way, so I packed everyone up and drove straight to the store to buy two pacifiers—one to give her, and one to store in the van.

—JOHN D'EREDITA
SYRACUSE, NEW YORK
19 12

I OFFERED A PACIFIER TO EACH BABY because I figured it would be an easier habit to break than a thumb. But guess what? That is really the baby's decision. All three of mine absolutely refused to use a pacifier.

—HEIDE A.W. KAMINSKI
TECUMSEH, MICHIGAN
18 15 6

• • • • • • • •

MY SON WAS THOROUGHLY ADDICTED TO HIS PACIFIER. To wean him off of it, we told him that when he turned three he would be too old for his pacifier, and because of this, it would break. The night before my son's third birthday my husband and I went around the house cutting off the tips of all the pacifiers. In the morning, my son ran up to me crying, "Mommy, Mommy! You were right! I'm three today and my pacifier is broken!" That was it. He never asked for it again.

—PAMELA BARTH
BAKERSFIELD, CALIFORNIA
20 17 3 9M

• • • • • • • •

THE FIRST NIGHT WE TOOK MY SON'S PACIFIER AWAY there was no argument or even crying. The next night we had 45 minutes of screaming and smashing the crib against the wall. The third night went without incident and he's been happily "binky"-free ever since.

—CHRISTINE BEIDEL
RUTHERFORD, NEW JERSEY
11 2

SOMETIMES GAS IS THE CULPRIT. Take a four-ounce bottle with drinking water in it, slightly warmed. Put in the tiniest pinch of baking soda—just a pinch—like, one sixteenth of a teaspoon or less. Shake it vigorously, and try to get the baby to drink a tablespoon. I did this with my son when he was two months old. I had to lay him down and make the droplets go into his mouth as he was yelling. About one teaspoon of swallowed water later, he let out a gigantic (for his tiny body) burp and was much, much better. No amount of back-patting, change of positions, attempts to nurse, singing, or handing him to others worked.

—*Melanie Watson*
Vernon, BC, Canada
4

For crying babies, be sure to check everything—teething, hunger, dirty diaper—then, resort to vacuuming, driving, or the swing. Music helps too.

—*E. Hirsh*
West Palm Beach, Florida
7

I USED TO PRETEND THAT A HIDDEN CAMERA was in the room with me and that I had to keep my cool in case they showed it on "Oprah" or something. It forced me say to myself, "Would I want other people to see how I am reacting right now?"

—*Wendy Snyder*
Westminster, Colorado
8 4

WHEN OUR DAUGHTER CRIED, we made sure nothing was seriously wrong, and then we'd put her in her bouncy chair, the crib, or the Pack-n-Play, and let her cry. Usually, she would calm herself down. But before we put her down, we would always hug her and tell her we loved her.

—*Anonymous*
Liverpool, New York
10 8

MY HUSBAND AND I FOUND ONLY TWO THINGS that worked to stop my daughter from crying. One was to put her in her car seat and drive around. The other was to take her into the laundry room, and turn the clothes dryer on. The heat combined with the humming sound calmed her down.

—*SANDI*
ALLENTOWN, PENNSYLVANIA
11

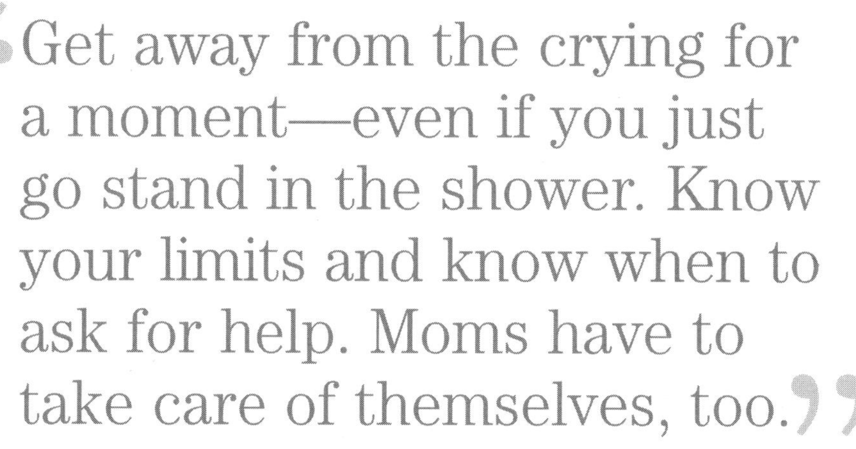
"Get away from the crying for a moment—even if you just go stand in the shower. Know your limits and know when to ask for help. Moms have to take care of themselves, too."

—*J.R.*
CHICAGO, ILLINOIS
21 18

THIS RUNS CONTRARY TO THE ADVICE my parents gave me, but I believe very strongly if your baby is crying, pick her up. Don't let her cry it out. Babies' wants are their needs. I don't think it's possible to spoil a baby—a toddler, yes, but not a baby.

—*MARY BRIGHT*
ALLENTOWN, PENNSYLVANIA
33 31

IF YOU CAN REMEMBER THAT BABIES are simply communicating the best way they can when they cry, you may be able to find the humor in it all. I think babies are so adorable when they make that crying face! So I laugh and it keeps my mood elevated and patient while I wait out the crying.

—*MONICA AND TODD DENNIS*
BRIDGEPORT, CONNECTICUT
4 6M

"Letting my son 'cry it out' was one of the most triumphant decisions I've made as a parent. It proved my theory that if you stop rewarding bad behavior, the behavior stops."

—*SARAH*
ST. LOUIS PARK, MINNESOTA
5

When you feel the anger and frustration building up inside you, walk away.

—*DAVID*
DENVER, COLORADO
11 9 4

THERE WERE TIMES WHEN MY BABY WOULD do nothing but scream and cry. I went berserk trying to figure out why. She was cleaned, fed and not hot or cold. Then my mother said, "Well, maybe she is teething." Sure enough, after I gave her teething balm, she stopped crying.

—*DAWN COLCLASURE-WILSON*
RANCHO MIRAGE, CALIFORNIA
2

THAT VOODOO THAT YOU DO

My son was so colicky that my wife and I barely slept for six weeks. Finally, my wife took him to a Cajun woman who laid him on his belly and tried to touch his right arm to his left leg, but couldn't. She told my wife this meant my son's intestines were deranged, which was causing him great pain, and that was why he was constantly crying.

The Cajun woman said a few prayers, then held my son upside down and shook him hard three times. When my wife came home she told me we had to continue doing this every morning for nine days before the sun comes up, I thought she was out of her mind. However, because I was at the end of my rope, I went along with it. I kid you not—on the ninth day, not only were his right arm and left foot able to touch, but he slept through the night.

I think people should resort to methods like this only as a last resort, once they've tried everything else medically possible. However, if you decide to try it, keep an open mind, because it really can work.

—Anthony Manuel
Kinder, Louisiana
17 14 11

CURING WHAT AILS YOU

When my daughter was a baby, my husband and I rocked her to sleep each night. It was a special time, but often when we tried to sneak her into her crib after she had fallen asleep, she would wake up again, screaming. So then we'd have to rock her to sleep again.

When she was a year old, I spoke with a pediatrician, who said we had to stop doing this, for our good and for hers. He said no matter how hard it was, we needed to put her in her crib and just let her cry.

The first night we did it, our daughter cried for a half hour. I cried too, as my husband and I sat downstairs and listened. But we didn't go to her. It was amazing: The second night she cried only for five minutes, and the third night she didn't cry at all. After a year of having such a hard time getting her to sleep, our daughter was "cured" in three nights!

—Sandi
Allentown, Pennsylvania
11

WHEN SHE CRIES AND THE REASON IS NOT OBVIOUS (she's not hungry, wet, tired, or sick), standing up and holding her while you bounce from one foot to another works 90 percent of the time.

—*ANONYMOUS*
ALAMEDA, CALIFORNIA
7M

• • • • • • • •

AFTER A COUPLE OF WEEKS OF nightly crying, with me trying everything from feeding to burping to rocking, I realized that the baby was just tired and everything I was doing to help her was actually making it worse. When I started putting her in her bassinet and just letting her fuss a little, she would fall asleep within five minutes. She was then consistently asleep by nine p.m. and could fall asleep on her own without crying at all.

—*SHAUNA FARRELL*
VANCOUVER, BC, CANADA
2 8M

Don't listen to the old wives' tales about how holding your baby too much spoils them. It doesn't spoil them. It makes them feel loved and babies need to feel loved.

—*GUADALUPE GOMEZ*
AZUSA, CALIFORNIA
36 34 31

• • • • • • • •

ROCK, NURSE, DANCE, WEAR A SLING, DRIVE in the car, administer gripe water and Simethicone drops. Different strategies work for different kids. Our son liked to be jogged around the room to music—particularly loud industrial music. He liked Ministry and Nine Inch Nails. And so do I.

—*MARRIT INGMAN*
AUSTIN, TEXAS
2

• • • • • • • •

WE SING AND DANCE WITH HER. We make the baby happy, we bounce her around a bit, and we move her legs like she's J. Lo—well, maybe her moves aren't as smooth, but once she's moving, she's happy.

—*ELIZABETH GIARMUNDEA*

TEETHING WISDOM

IF YOUR BABY IS TEETHING AND KEEPING THE WHOLE FAMILY UP at night crying because of it, rub a little (just a little) whiskey on his or her gums to numb the pain. It works wonders. You might want to rub a little on your own gums as well.

—JILL FULLEN
SWISSVALE, PENNSYLVANIA
24

• • • • • • • •

ONE TIME, WHEN OUR SON WAS TEETHING, WE PUT HIM in a stroller and wheeled him around the house. As long as we moved, he was fine. As soon as we stopped, he'd cry again. Everyone took turns wheeling him around. We have a really cute video of our baby with his grandpa walking behind him, and the dog walking behind them. It was a parade!

—LINDA BOWER
LOVELAND, COLORADO
9 6

• • • • • • • •

FOR TEETHING, NUMSIT USED TO WORK WELL. I would also give my babies frozen rattles to chew on.

—NOLA SMITH
TAMPA, FLORIDA
41 35

WHEN YOUR BABY IS CRYING and they stop for a moment to see if they can hear you coming, it's probably not that bad. They are just learning the fine points of manipulating their environment (and conditioning you at the same time).

—*R.A.*
CEDAR RAPIDS, IOWA
24 22

• • • • • • • •

I USED TO HOLD MY SON AND DANCE HIM all around the room, singing either to music on the radio, or to songs I had stored in my head. (One night I sang all the Herman's Hermits songs I could remember, which turned out to be a surprising amount!) We'd dance for hours at a time. I really miss those days.

—*STEPHANIE WOLFE*
GROTON, CONNECTICUT
23M

• • • • • • • •

SOMETIMES, IT'S OK TO LET A BABY CRY. Babies have to exercise their lungs sometimes. With my oldest son, it was simple. I'd put him in his bed, check if he was hungry, check for a tummy ache, and so on. If he kept crying, I shut the door, I let him cry and I didn't let it bother me.

—*THOMAS M.W. "MIKE" DOWNS*
SYRACUSE, NEW YORK
20 16 13 10

• • • • • • • •

TO SOOTHE OUR CHILDREN IN THEIR CRIBS, we found a vibrating attachment at Wal-Mart that clipped on to a crib or bassinet. Switching it on created a gentle movement that soothed the children—especially when they were tired.

—*ELAINE MCGUIRE*
WINDSOR, COLORADO
20 18 6 4

To stop our babies from crying, my husband would place the baby across his lap, face down, and give the kid a back rub. Worked almost every time.

—*V.B.*
DOHA, QATAR
23 21 14

INFANT INFO

Kangaroo Care is a Bolivian technique for soothing babies with skin-to-skin contact. Parents are encouraged to hold fussy newborns against their bare chests to calm them.

I SPEND A LOT OF TIME WALKING with my son around the house to keep him from crying. Sometimes, though, I have to set him down and walk outside for five minutes just so I do not have to keep listening. That little break helps a lot.

—*Michelle M.*
Oostburg, Wisconsin
2 2M

• • • • • • • •

MIRACLE CURE FOR COLIC: FENNEL TEA! Our daughter suffered terribly from colic. She was constantly crying and screaming. Finally, a nutritionist recommended that we give her a few teaspoons of fennel tea. The colic stopped immediately and has not returned. We had tried so many different medicines, but to no avail. We're so happy with this natural remedy!

—*W.S.B.*
Houston, Texas
6 3 2 2M

• • • • • • • •

I HAVE FOUND THAT WHEN NOTHING ELSE will work, get out the Tylenol. If you are against that, then try sleeping upright with the baby on you in a recliner. That helps sometimes.

—*Tonya Lee*
Mount Airy, Maryland
8 5

• • • • • • • •

A GREAT TIME TO TAKE A SHOWER is just after you put the baby to bed—and the baby's still crying. Not only will this prevent you from running to pick up the baby when what he really needs is sleep, it's doubly relaxing because: a) it's a hot shower, and b) you can't hear the crying.

—*Heidi*
Chicago, Illinois
14 11 6

10

The Real World: Work, Family, and Life

Who goes off to work? Who stays at home with the baby? Who cooks dinner? How do you pick a daycare provider? How can you possibly leave your little darling with a stranger? How do you keep it all straight and get it all done? The answers are here.

"GUILT" IS NOT THE PROPER word to describe what it feels like to leave your child all day. The flip side is, a lot of women seem to go a bit batty being home all day with youngsters without having some sort of adult interaction and stimulation.

—*BARBARA*

GET A SALES JOB SO THAT YOU CAN WORK FROM HOME!

—*J.H.*
MILL VALLEY, CALIFORNIA
9

WORK TOGETHER. Raising a child, especially during those first years, should be a team effort. Gone are the days when the mother took on all the responsibilities of child rearing. It's hard work, with many challenges and unbelievable rewards, all of which should be shared by both parents.

—*LAURA KRONEN*
NEW YORK, NEW YORK
15M

It's very hard to go from working full-time to staying home all day. A spouse needs to be supportive and help out with diapers and baths and other household chores. Mine doesn't.

—*M.*
EDGEWATER, MARYLAND
4 3M

• • • • • • • •

WHEN I GET HOME, I PRETTY MUCH GIVE ALL my attention to the kids because I don't get to see them all day. The other stuff you think is important—work around the house—can wait. It's not as important when you put it in perspective with how fleeting those moments with your kids are.

—*KEN BECKERING*
SYRACUSE, NEW YORK
5 2

• • • • • • • •

WHEN SELECTING A DAYCARE PROVIDER, drop in unexpectedly to see what the place is really like. Look for a facility that is clean and where the children are happy. Watch how the caregivers interact with the children. Ask lots of questions. Don't worry about asking something that will offend them—the treatment of your child is more important. Find out the beliefs of the caregivers, how they discipline, their teaching styles and how they feel about issues that are important to you. If you have any doubts, it probably isn't the place to take your most precious treasure.

—*STACEY HATFIELD*
ANAHUAC, TEXAS
4

GO TO ANY LENGTHS NECESSARY to have someone you know watch your children. When we needed a person to care for our children, we went to the wife of the deacon who married us even though she lives some distance away. For us, the security and welfare of our kids was the number one priority.

—*RICK BARBERO*
GAITHERSBURG, MARYLAND
12 5

"Babies make you add weird 'eeee' sounds to the end of your words. 'The doggie went to sleepy.' Be careful when in professional settings to remove the 'eeee' from your words."

—*TILLY*
CHAMPAIGN, ILLINOIS
15

IT IS ABSOLUTELY POSSIBLE TO HAVE A CAREER and raise a family. But a woman has to make the decision that she is going to work hard to be a mother to her baby and pursue her career. Every day I asked myself if I had been a good mother to my baby and done a good job at work. Yes, this is difficult, but it can be done.

—*PAT Q.T.*
OAKLAND, CALIFORNIA
32 27

Get a nanny.

—*SHARON MUALEM*
ATLANTA, GEORGIA
4 1

YOU MIGHT BE SURPRISED TO DISCOVER that it is possible to stay home with your kids, if that's what you want to do. I am a scientist, so I had a hard time imagining how I could possibly work from home. But I do! I work from home as a consultant for pharmaceutical companies and health insurance companies, do medical writing, and lecture at a university. If you can be creative, there are lots of opportunities out there to work from home. You can start your own business, do Tupperware, the sky's the limit. I figure if I can do it, anyone can!

—*Kelly Karpa*
Pennsylvania
5 3

Go through an accredited babysitting agency. But still go with your gut instincts. If you think something is not quite right about a sitter, you're probably right.

—*Lisa Armony*
Sherman Oaks, California
5 2

WHEN BOTH PARENTS WORK, it must be a shared responsibility. At first, I'd stay at work a little late—just 30 minutes longer than usual. I'd come home and see my wife's stress. She had picked up the kids and gone home. Our daughter needed her diaper changed. Dinner needed to be started. And our son was crying for attention. We decided that we needed to come home at the same time. Then, each of us could handle some of the responsibilities.

—*Chris Graham*
Syracuse, New York
4 1

I STAYED HOME WHEN MY DAUGHTER was growing up. I thought that it was important for me or my husband to be home, but we made some tough choices to do that. It took us longer to save for a house, for instance. We lived in a one-bedroom, third-floor apartment until our daughter went to kindergarten.

—*Betty*
Lower Saucony, Pennsylvania
34

THE FIRST TIME I LEFT MY BABY SON with a sitter, I became aware that Mother Nature controls more than I suspected. The entire time I was away from my baby, my mind and body were aware every second that a) my son was somewhere else, and b) I didn't know if he was perfectly OK. Even though the sitter was a trusted employee of my husband's, I could not shake the constant feeling that I should be back home with him. Consequently, my forays from home were brief initially.

—JANNY TANG
SANTA CRUZ, CALIFORNIA
31

"Get dads involved early. They aren't trying to escape from helping; they are just overwhelmed and don't know where to begin."

—ERICA CAMARA
WHITEMAN AIR FORCE BASE, MISSOURI
17M

AFTER HAVING OUR SECOND CHILD I went back to work full-time, so we hired a nanny who's at our home 50 hours a week. Mothering my children is the highest priority, so yes, I wish I spent more time at home. And yet I also find work stimulating, challenging and rewarding.

—A.D.
SAN FRANCISCO, CALIFORNIA
3 1

IT TAKES TWO

AT FIRST, MY WIFE GOT IRRITATED WITH ME when I would have her take the kids every time I needed to get something done. She pointed out that she didn't have that luxury during the week when I was at work, and I should learn to deal with kids and life simultaneously. So, I've had to become more proficient at multitasking—a kid on the lap while at the computer, feeding the kids while talking on the phone.

—*J.R.*
CHICAGO, ILLINOIS
4 2 1

• • • • • • • •

WHEN IT WAS JUST OUR FIRST CHILD, I did more of my share of housekeeping than I had normally done. (Of course, this would mean I had done something to begin with, so anything at that point was an improvement.) But housework was only half of what I needed to do to be helpful. You also have to make sure you're there emotionally, with as much understanding as you can give.

—*DAVID E. LISS*
PENNINGTON, NEW JERSEY
4 1

• • • • • • • •

WHEN OUR CHILDREN WERE BORN, I HAD A JOB that required inordinately long hours. But, when I finally did get home, I made it a point to plunge in. Sure, I was tired. But what about my wife, who had coped all day? I'd help with the baths, feedings, diaper changing, story time. I'd take care of them on my days off so my wife could get out by herself. It made a huge difference in my wife being able to survive the rigors of motherhood, and in my appreciation of her skills and talents in dealing with it all.

—*DOUGLAS S. LOONEY*
BOULDER, COLORADO
37 34

I TOOK A ONE-YEAR SABBATICAL WHEN MY DAUGHTER was about three and my son was a year. I was working on my own projects, but I took total responsibility for picking them up, dropping them off, taking them to the doctor. It was tremendous. The best part of it was developing a relationship with my kids.

—*ANONYMOUS*
BETHESDA, MARYLAND
9 6

• • • • • • • • •

WHEN I GOT HOME FROM WORK, THE FIRST THING I DID was pick up my boy to give my wife a break. When I did this on a regular basis, she stopped nagging me about petty little things. It's a very worthwhile exchange.

—*ROBERT HARRIS*
LOS ANGELES, CALIFORNIA
26 17

• • • • • • • • •

SINCE I DID CHILDCARE WHILE WORKING FROM HOME on weekdays, my husband had full childcare responsibility (except for nursing, of course!) when he came home from work at night, and on weekends. Plus, he made dinner when he got home from work. When he told a female acquaintance about our arrangement, she said, "But you've been working all day! You need to rest!" His reply: "So has she—at two jobs!" Wonderful man!

—*KATHARINE O'MOORE-KLOPF*
EAST SETAUKET, NEW YORK
21 9 2

I FOUND OUR BABYSITTER THROUGH SOMEONE who used to clean my house. I trusted my former housekeeper's opinion, but I still did my research. I met my babysitter several times before we hired her, and I watched her interact with my children. She was good natured and made direct eye contact. Plus I knew she had raised four children of her own.

—*LISA ANGELETTIE, M.S.W.*
ENGLEWOOD, NEW JERSEY
5 3 2

Spend a lot of time with your children, even if you're a working mother. Quality time with your child is extremely important. These are the most influential years of their life.

—*MICHELLE HIRSCH*
ATLANTA, GEORGIA
8

IF YOU WANT TO WORK FROM HOME, plan on getting some extra childcare, even if it's only a teenage helper to keep an eye on your baby while you work in another room. I had planned on working from home after my baby was born, squeezing it in during my daughter's naps. But I discovered that naptimes are about the only time you can get anything done: housework, cooking, sleeping, relaxing, reading. Forcing myself to hop on the computer during those precious few hours when I wanted to do everything else was difficult.

—*MELODY WARNICK*
ST. GEORGE, UTAH
2

PLACES TO FIND GOOD SITTERS ARE CHURCHES and universities. The university in our town has a list of students in child and human development classes who want to babysit because they need the experience for their majors. Two college girls that we found this way ended up having roommates who also became good babysitters for our kids.

—*JILL*
FORT COLLINS, COLORADO
7 3

After they've just eaten, watch out! I came home from work one day at lunchtime wearing a pure white uniform. I picked up my two-week old son and started playing with him. All of a sudden, I felt this warmth all over my chest. He had completely soiled my shirt, and I barely had enough time to change clothes before getting back to the office.

—Mark Scott
Safford, Arizona
16 13

I took my wife to Paris as a surprise Valentine's Day present after our daughter was born. We left the baby with my mom. We called from the road on the way to the airport, from the airport, from the plane, when we arrived, from the hotel. I am proud to report we didn't call to check on her from the Eiffel Tower. But we probably talked about whether we should.

—Allan Jaffe
Petaluma, California
21 6

For the first week after my wife returned to work we went together to take our daughter to and from daycare. We did that more for us than for her, so that we would both know the routine. I felt very sad to leave her because I didn't know how she would react to the new situation. It turns out she was very happy to be there, but I was sad.

—Daniel H. Aminoff
Alexandria, Virginia
5M

My husband takes care of the house so it doesn't look like a bomb went off, and I'm more involved with our baby. Our load is balanced right now.

—M. DeJong
Fairfax, California
5W

TRYING TO BALANCE WORK WITH FAMILY, I just got used to being exhausted. I still have visions of myself driving to work in the morning at about seven a.m., having just dropped off two kids at two different places and feeling so tired it was hard to believe I was just starting the day. But I did fine at work once I was there, and I managed to handle everything, so I think we just adapt.

—*BARBARA STEWART*
SEATTLE, WASHINGTON
20 17

"We set up a system to reduce stress: Every night, one parent was allowed one hour to go shopping, take a bath, get some exercise, whatever. The next night was the other person's turn."

—*MICHAEL*
ST. PAUL, MINNESOTA
11 5

MY HUSBAND WAS EXCELLENT ABOUT HELPING me out. In fact, he seemed to make a better mother than I did when it came to handling the feedings/changings so expertly!

—*BEV PORTER*
COLORADO SPRINGS, COLORADO
14 11

AFTER MY FIRST NANNY WANTED TO BE PAID two full weeks while our family was on vacation without her, I decided to make a "nanny handbook." It spelled out everything—from what the baby could eat to how much TV the other kids could watch. There was even a section in it that entitled me to three "free days" where I could cancel the nanny if my mother or mother-in-law wanted to take the kids for a day. Nannies had to agree to the conditions and sign a "contract." I also made the nannies keep a logbook of the activities around the house so I could see what my kids were doing. That way, I knew what to expect when I was home.

—*SUZANNE DAUGHERTY*
ARLINGTON HEIGHTS, ILLINOIS
7 5 2

WHEN I WENT BACK TO WORK after four months, things became intensely stressful. I was doing most of the work at home in addition to working a full day. My husband and I snapped at one another and started taking each other for granted. After a huge falling out—which we never had before—he realized that he had to pitch in more. Now he helps out so much and a lot of the burden has been lifted from me. It's all about finding the balance of time for myself, time for our daughter, and time for my husband. I also needed to learn to ask for help and not be Supermom, and not feel guilty. It was a huge maturation process for me.

—*A.S.*
11M

INFANT INFO

A Census Bureau report shows that between 1994 and 2002, there was an 18-percent increase in the number of stay-at-home dads.

ALL NEW MOTHERS SHOULD FORCE THEMSELVES to be apart from their babies sometime within the first six months. I didn't trust anyone to take care of my firstborn and I refused to leave him with anybody. Then, my son had to get his tonsils taken out, and moms weren't allowed to stay at the hospital, so we were separated for two whole nights. It was so traumatic that I went home and cried my eyes out.

—*JANIS HACKETT*
CENTENNIAL, COLORADO
36 32 26 24

It's amazing how many things you can get done with one hand. You really master that while you're holding a baby in one arm!

—*MICHELE CONTIS*
FAIRFAX, CALIFORNIA
11W

• • • • • • • • •

IF PEOPLE CAN AFFORD IT, I REALLY RECOMMEND one parent work only part-time. When my youngest son was born, I went back to work full-time right away. It was so hard, sometimes I wonder how I got through it. A few months later, I had the opportunity to change jobs and work only part time. When I asked my husband about it, he said, "Do you even need to ask?" There was no question; it was the best thing for our family.

—*TRUDY*
PERKASIE, PENNSYLVANIA
59 57 46 40

• • • • • • • • •

WHEN IT COMES TO BABYSITTING, I am appalled at how little most people are willing to pay for it. You are leaving your precious child's very life in the hands of someone else; is this not worth more than the price of a couple of movie tickets? We overpaid greatly on purpose because we wanted her sitters to know how much we valued their time and skills.

—*KATHLEEN JUN MAGYAR*
DALLAS, TEXAS
18

WHEN YOU'RE CHOOSING A BABYSITTER, have him/her over to your house for an hour or so while you're there. Stay close enough that you can hear and/or see what's going on, but far enough away that your child and the babysitter don't include you in their interaction. You'll have a pretty good sense of whether it's the right fit or not.

—*DEBORAH FISHER*
FORT WASHINGTON, PENNSYLVANIA
9M

"I didn't expect to be so bored at times. Shaking a rattle at the baby isn't the most stimulating of pastimes."

—*DEANA KRAUSE*
CHICAGO, ILLINOIS
11 9

TWO WEEKS AFTER MY C-SECTION my company told me they needed me to come to Hawaii to do an advertisement. They told me to bring my baby and husband, so I said, "Absolutely! I'm there, no problem." I was probably still doped up at the time and thinking that I was healed. Twenty-four hours later I was in the most excruciating pain and somehow, later that week, I was supposed to be hiking down cliffs to oversee a photo shoot. There was just no way.

—*MARGARET KEENE*
HERMOSA BEACH, CALIFORNIA
8M

HERE'S MY ABSOLUTE NUMBER ONE piece of advice for stay-at-home parents: Get together with other stay-at-home parents! The isolation of being alone with a baby can drive you crazy. Finding those parents and sharing the joys, stresses, excitement, and challenges of parenting is the best thing you can do for yourself.

—*EVAN WEISSMAN*
OAKLAND, CALIFORNIA
6 3

My husband and I laugh about how two intelligent people can carry on a conversation over dinner about poopy and super soaker diapers.

—*MICHELLE LEWIS*
PLANTATION, FLORIDA
2M

I MADE SURE THAT LEAVING MY DAUGHTER at day care the first time wasn't horrible by making sure I didn't do it when I was returning to work. I did a couple practice runs where I just left her for three hours or so. I was working from home during that time, so I also had things to keep me busy and not focused on worrying about her.

—*JULIE KIND*
ARLINGTON, VIRGINIA
6M

I RUN THE HOUSEHOLD, AS FAR AS LAUNDRY, cooking, cleaning, etc. My husband, however, is very involved with playtime, bath time, diapering, feeding and all aspects of childcare. On the weekends, we share all responsibilities and he is a very hands-on daddy. He'll also spend alone time with each of the children. I think this makes for everyone being happier.

—*VANESSA WILKINSON*
COLORA, MARYLAND
3 5M

MAKE SURE THE BABYSITTER has good references and does a lot with the kids, not just stick them in front of the TV. The one I have now takes them outside every day (weather permitting), does art projects, reads books, and teaches them things.

—*LAUREN HIDDEN*
NEW CUMBERLAND, PENNSYLVANIA
4 2

"I felt guilty about not spending more time with my baby. Then I realized that the quantity of time spent with my child was not as important as the quality of our experiences."

—*SUZANNE*
FORT COLLINS, COLORADO
4

I'VE STAYED AT HOME WITH MY KIDS until they were five years old, independent and off to kindergarten. Then I went back to work. Parenting is a unique experience; you can always work, so I really cherished those years that they were infants.

—*GLORIA RIVERA*
BURLINGAME, CALIFORNIA
21 20 16 10 1M

PICTURE, VIDEO, AND THE INTERNET

TAKE A PICTURE OF THE BABY EACH MONTH on the date of his birth for the whole first year. I also try to tape a 10-minute video of my son once a week, nothing special; I just film him throughout the day doing whatever he's doing.

—ROBYN
BIGLERVILLE, PENNSYLVANIA
1

• • • • • • • •

WHEN YOU DECIDE IT'S TIME TO TAKE BABY to the photographer's studio to get his or her picture taken, do it after the baby has eaten and napped. Otherwise they can be all fussy and fidgety. They tend to be much more cooperative if their belly is full and they're not tired.

—ANONYMOUS
BRUNSWICK, OHIO
5 4

• • • • • • • •

INSTEAD OF TRYING TO WAIT FOR ONE GREAT VIDEO moment, take lots of little videos of everyday things. After a year, you'll have all sorts of great footage that you can edit together—the baby rolling over or eating, or even just sitting and crying. It will be a great thing to look back at when your child is older.

—ELLIS
SEATTLE, WASHINGTON
1

• • • • • • • •

FOR A GOOD PICTURE, GET CLOSE. For a better picture, get closer.

—M. ALLEN
ATLANTA, GEORGIA
6 3

A PROFESSIONAL PHOTOGRAPHER ONCE TOLD ME that when you take still portraits of your kids, keep their eyes in the upper third of the picture because it balances the photo and makes the kid the center of attention.

—Stephanie Ismert
Centennial, Colorado
8 6 1

• • • • • • • •

AT LEAST TWO PEOPLE ARE REQUIRED to take a good baby picture—one to hold the baby and one to make funny faces and to push the button. I have found that raising the baby up in the air makes him smile, so my wife gets in position underneath and we get good Superbaby shots.

—Dan Dupont
Arlington, Virginia
6 3 3M

• • • • • • • •

THERE ARE SEVERAL ONLINE PHOTO SITES, which make it easy to share photos. Simply download your digital photos from your camera to the computer and upload them to any photo site of your choosing. Many of them allow you free storage (as long as you place print orders) so you'll always have an extra backup. You can share them with anyone who has an e-mail address and they too can order their own photos.

—Adriane
Ft. Lauderdale, Florida
1

• • • • • • • •

WE USED A WEB SITE TO MAKE THE BIRTH announcement. It had several pictures and information about our daughter, including where her name came from.

—Elizabeth Edwardsen
South Portland, Maine
7

I HAD MY CHILDREN WITH ME ALL DAY LONG. My husband would come home, and I'd want him to take the baby because I needed a break. They'd start crying and instead of trying to deal with it and play with them or walk with them or rock them or get on the floor with them, he'd say, "They don't like me." Then he'd hand them back. He'd change poopy diapers with no complaint. But aside from that, it was hard for him.

—ANDREA
GRAND LAKE, COLORADO
9 5

• • • • • • • •

ONE PARENT SHOULD WORK FROM HOME. My husband is a writer, so he was often at home and available to help with our daughter. I don't know how I would have handled life if he wasn't available to help during the day. While a babysitter or nanny may still be necessary, the working-at-home parent can be a secure presence to the child.

—E.G.
NEW HAVEN, CONNECTICUT
20

• • • • • • • •

AFTER EACH KID IS BORN, IT'S ALWAYS HARD when I go back to my job. My husband works days and I work nights as a pharmacist, so we've been able to share duties and avoid most paid childcare. But it's still difficult not being home. I get calls like, "Don't worry, honey, but where is the medical insurance card?" So many of the calls start with, "Don't worry, honey, but . . ."

—PILAR SHOAP
ABINGDON, MARYLAND
7 4 2 3M

SET THE WORKLOAD BALANCE UP FRONT. Don't expect your husband to be considerate; don't expect him to be the one to get up in the middle of the night. I told him I needed time for myself on weekends. That caused a lot of fights. He would say, "I work full-time." I would respond with, "What do you think I'm doing?"

—ISABELLA
SANTA CRUZ, CALIFORNIA
18M

I MADE A MISTAKE WHEN MY KIDS were younger by not spending enough time with them. If you work all day long, cut down to half a day or you'll miss out on a lot. It's beautiful to be with a child.

—B.
LOS ANGELES, CALIFORNIA

WITH THREE KIDS ALL UNDER the age of five, there was no such thing as sharing the load— the load was all mine! My husband had just started his own business and was gone day and night, 24/7. Some days my nerves would be totally shot by 10:00 in the morning. When I did get time to myself I would indulge in an alcoholic beverage (usually a beer), and write in my journal. This was one of the things that saved my sanity. I also had a friend that was a stay-at-home mom. We would call each other up while making our dinner and having our drinks together over the phone. It was nice to know someone else was experiencing the same frustration, loneliness and isolation.

—S.C.
BRAMPTON, ONTARIO, CANADA
17 15 12

Don't get rid of your hip clothes once you stop fitting into them. They will serve as reminders of your days of hipness.

—ANONYMOUS
STOCKDALE, TEXAS
2 7M

LIKE EVERYTHING ELSE, WE TRIED TO SPLIT the workload evenly. Since my wife is a light sleeper, and it takes a lot to wake me up, she responded to his late night cries most of the time. However, on those occasions where she was too exhausted or simply didn't feel like getting up, a sharp elbow to my sides was usually enough to get me out of bed.

—*JOHN RODGERS*
SEATTLE, WASHINGTON
9

If you're moody, talk about it with your husband. The more you talk, the more he'll understand.

—*TICIA*
SYRACUSE, NEW YORK
6 4

DON'T BE AFRAID TO REACH OUT FOR HELP. We hired a "doula," which is the German term for someone who helps with the baby, cooking and cleaning. She's a nanny, a housekeeper and can do anything we need, from preparing a meal to changing the baby.

—*G.P.*
MINNEAPOLIS, MINNESOTA
2M

AS MY HUSBAND WAS THE ONE GOING OUT to work each day and I was a stay-at-home mom, I did most of the workload. Organization is the key to it all, as is planning ahead. I keep a calendar on my computer and on my fridge to help keep me on top of things.

—*LYNDA DIFRANCESCO*
RALEIGH, NORTH CAROLINA
2 2M

DON'T STOP DOING THE THINGS YOU LOVE TO DO. I still shop, go to restaurants, dance and travel, yet I am a mom.

—*L.G.*
WEST NEW YORK, NEW JERSEY
2

BE FLEXIBLE. I try to plan out my days, but with a baby sometimes it just doesn't work. Each night I make a list of the things I hope to do the next day. It makes me feel really good when I check things off of it. But it doesn't always work out that way, so I've learned to be flexible.

—JILL
SHOEMAKERSVILLE, PENNSYLVANIA
11M

• • • • • • • •

I FOUND THAT IT WAS ACTUALLY EASIER to work from home in the first month than it was in the following months. While the baby was sleeping I could do a lot. In later months, when the baby needed more interaction, it was harder to get anything done.

—BRETTE SEMBER
CLARENCE, NEW YORK
12 6

• • • • • • • •

IF YOU'RE THE STAY-AT-HOME PARENT, you will be doing a lot more. There's no way around it. I work from home so I feel like I get stuck with most of the housework, because I can do bits here and there throughout the day. I feel like I'm never really "off," but it's hard to ask him to do more when he comes home from work and he's tired, too.

—SHAUNA FARRELL
VANCOUVER, BC, CANADA
2 8M

• • • • • • • •

LIVE CLOSE TO YOUR PARENTS OR SOMEONE that can babysit for free. It will save you so much money in the long run, and probably save your relationship as well, because you will feel like you can go out together, alone, more often.

—TOCCA
BROOKLYN, NEW YORK

ONCE I WENT BACK TO WORK, we had to take turns doing everything. I would do a load of laundry in the morning and he would put one in at night. If I cooked, he cleaned the kitchen. If I swept the floors, he vacuumed. While I nursed, he would get her bath stuff ready. We had to learn how to work as a team.

—STACEY HATFIELD
ANAHUAC, TEXAS
4

I WENT TO MY HAIRDRESSER THE OTHER DAY with my hair pulled back in a banana clip and she said, "You look like such a mom!" Inside, I thought, "Oh, God, no! Not a mom!" I guess the moral of the story is that if you want to stay cool, don't wear banana clips. Or overalls.

—STEPHANIE ISMERT
CENTENNIAL, COLORADO
8 6 1

GET A BABYSITTER ASAP—within six months. My spouse and I go out one night a week together and we each get "a night off."

—TRACEY G.
SAN FRANCISCO, CALIFORNIA
3

TO HELP ME GET MY LIFE BACK, I had to find a way to get together with adult friends and not talk about babies. I started a mom's group where we talk about world issues, to keep our brains active.

—KATRINA CURRIER
SAN FRANCISCO, CALIFORNIA
17M

CELL PHONES CAN BE A REAL LIFELINE to adult contact. I loved talking to friends while I was pushing the stroller when he was just a baby. And I figured if I wasn't on the phone, we would just be walking along in silence. So at least this way he was hearing my voice.

—K.C.
SAN FRANCISCO, CALIFORNIA
2

• • • • • • • •

FOR GOD'S SAKE, THEY'RE CUTE—just watch them. I think there is this feeling that everything has to be documented—you know, the first haircut, the first everything. And that documentation becomes more important than the event itself. I think a lot of people miss a lot of things because they're so busy taking pictures they don't actually see what's going on.

—DEB
ORONO, MAINE
18

• • • • • • • •

I E-MAIL MY PARENTS ROUTINELY about milestones and funny things that happen. My mother, in particular, loves them. She's far away and, like me, on the computer all day, so e-mails about her grandkids are absolute treasures. What's more, these little e-mails and the responses they elicit make great baby book fodder. I'm notoriously bad at keeping up with such books, so I hoard e-mails and print out the ones about the kids for inclusion.

—DAN DUPONT
ARLINGTON, VIRGINIA
6 3 3M

WHEN MY DAUGHTER WAS BORN I LAUNCHED a "family news" Web site. I made it funny! And silly! And cute! But not too silly or cute. And I gave it video and picture galleries. In short, it was a place where my family and friends could log on, and witness the growth of our daughter, and later, our son. I wrote mercifully short news articles on developments in their lives, and funny articles on how parenthood had changed me and my wife. The other day I sat down with my daughter, now five, and showed her all the video, pictures and stories we have archived about her and her brother. She loved it, and it was a great way to relive memories.

—JWAIII
ATLANTA, GEORGIA
5 2

WHEN PEOPLE SAY THEY WANT TO SEE YOUR BABY pictures, they want to see one picture. They do not want to look through 10 albums with a thousand pictures each.

—DEB
ORONO, MAINE
18

11

Getting Out: Entertainment and Trips

No matter how overwhelmed you are by the idea of packing up strollers, diapers, food, toys, etc., the fact is, the time will come for you to take the baby out of the house. It might be to the park, it might be on a car trip, or it might be (brave soul) on an airplane. Not sure you can pull it off? Here's some useful advice, as well as some suggestions for entertaining baby at home on those days you just don't feel ready to meet the world.

WHENEVER YOU LEAVE THE HOUSE with kids, pack a snack to take with you wherever you go. Cheerios and animal crackers work well. And when I have enough time to think ahead, I pack cut up vegetables.

—*J. McNally*
Loveland, Colorado
9 7 16M

TAKE THEM TO THE PARK. THAT'S HOW YOU WEAR THEM OUT!

—*Tabitha Mott*
Cheyenne, Wyoming
10 7 5.5M

WHEN GOING SOMEWHERE WITH BABY, find the priority entrance. Most museums, restaurants, etc., have a priority entrance so people with special needs and babies don't have to wait in line. Find it and use it! It will make your life so much easier.

—L.C.
PITTSBURGH, PENNSYLVANIA
6 5

Having babies didn't seem to stop our vacations. We took our babies just about anywhere. Maybe that's why my girls like to travel to this day!

—DEE
OAK LAWN, ILLINOIS
29 24

• • • • • • • •

IT'S NOT WORTH TRYING TO TEACH a baby to play well with other children. They simply don't have the capacity to understand concepts like taking turns or sharing till they're toddlers, and even then it's tough. Just let them play near other kids and keep them from killing each other. Our kids turned out great that way, and now that they're older, they play just fine with others, despite the lack of early training.

—STEPH D.
BALTIMORE, MARYLAND
18 15 13

• • • • • • • •

A FEW YEARS AGO, I WAS ON THE HIGHWAY when there was a car accident down the road that backed up traffic for miles. I sat in that car for several hours. It was such a long time I fell asleep. Now that I have kids, I think back to that day and wonder what I would have done if they had been in the car with me. That's why everywhere I go, even if it's only a few miles away, I bring snacks to eat and water to drink. Just in case!

—ANGELA
BETHLEHEM, PENNSYLVANIA
5 -5W

WE HAVE A TAPE THAT'S BEEN PLAYING NON-STOP in the car's cassette player for two years. I think it's called something like, "The Best of Head, Shoulders, Knees and Toes." That falsetto kid won't shut up. He's on every song and for a climax he brings in the rest of the helium gang—just wonderful.

—B.P.
ORLANDO, FLORIDA
21M 7M

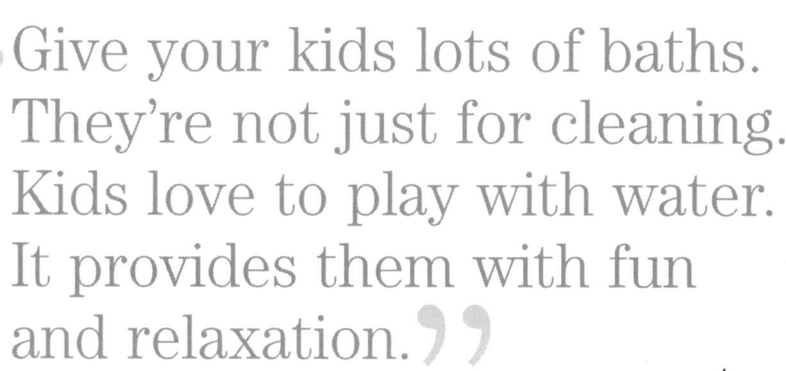

"Give your kids lots of baths. They're not just for cleaning. Kids love to play with water. It provides them with fun and relaxation."

—MEGAN
FORT COLLINS, COLORADO
3 9M

Make sure you have an extra set of clothes in the car for your kids, because they always get dirty.

—VERONICA
LOVELAND, COLORADO
4 3 1

I JOINED MOTHERS & MORE (a national organization with local chapters, http://www.mothersandmore.org) to socialize with other moms and have my son participate in playgroups. They have something similar to a babysitting co-op. I watch another member's child one night and she will watch mine another night, free of charge. My son is in trusted hands and gets to play with a familiar friend.

—LESLIE BUNDY
WAUKESHA, WISCONSIN
1

JUST DO IT!

It is scary taking your newborn out. I worried—do I have everything I need? What if he screams in public? What if I have to nurse? Don't all these idiots on the road realize I am carrying precious cargo in this car? Slow down!

But you have to get out, get over the fears, get used to being in public with your little one. It will do you a world of good and make you proud that you are able to go it alone with just your newborn to that grocery store! What an accomplishment!

—*Sheena Krock*
Kunkletown, Pennsylvania
14M

• • • • • • • •

Take your child with you when you go places. From the beginning, from those first weeks, we took our daughter with us everywhere. Now she's very relaxed when we all go out. She is very used to it. She's not fussy at all.

—*April*
Fort Collins, Colorado
5M

WHAT HELPS ME THE MOST IS TO HAVE SOMEONE with me when I go somewhere, to have that extra set of eyes to help me watch my kids. I usually ask my good friend or my children's grandma to come along on outings.

—*JESSICA*
MILLIKEN, COLORADO
2 3M

"Rather than just sitting at home with my son on weekends, where he can sometimes be fussy, I usually take him on errands. To him a trip to the hardware store is one big adventure."

—*JON*
BIGLERVILLE, PENNSYLVANIA
1

TRY TO HAVE MIXED-GENDER PLAYGROUPS for your little babies and toddlers. They start to play differently later on, and it's harder to have boys and girls together, but when they're really young, they can play very well with kids of the opposite sex and I think it helped my daughter be comfortable around boys as she was growing up.

—*N. CLARK*
HOUSTON, TEXAS
15

AS SOON AS YOU THINK YOUR BABY IS READY for it you should arrange a play-date with a friend's or relative's young child. It really helps a child's development to interact with children their own age. They can learn to share and work together to solve little problems and challenges. It is especially important if your child is an only child.

—*DON RODGERS*
NORTH HUNTINGDON, PENNSYLVANIA
17 14

Get down on the floor and play with your kid. Think like a kid. Move like a kid. Adjust your life to be more in tune with your kid.

—*BRITT STROMBERG*
CAMANO ISLAND, WASHINGTON
11M

JOIN A PLAYGROUP! It helps keep you sane. I really enjoy both aspects of being part of a playgroup. I'm a stay-at-home mom, so my children normally wouldn't get much social interaction. But they get to make friends in a playgroup. And I really appreciate the other parents in the group. We can gab and cry on each other's shoulders!

—*MELISSA GROOM*
FORT COLLINS, COLORADO
2 5M

I SEE SO MANY PARENTS TAKE their kids places with no toys to play with and then wonder why their kids act up! Even when my daughter was a baby, I kept a big basket of toys in the car at all times. Then when we needed to go someplace, such as to a friend's house or a doctor's office, I'd haul the basket inside. Friends comment on how well-behaved and well-entertained Rachel always is. It's so simple: I think it's because she always has something to keep her occupied.

—*CAROL GILMORE*
EASTON, PENNSYLVANIA
6

I PARTICIPATED IN A PLAYGROUP to provide my child with an "extended family." The great thing was having a support group of parents. Plus, no matter what age or stage my child was at, there was always somebody else in the group who had been through it already.

—*DONA LESSIN*
NEW YORK, NEW YORK
32

"Playgrounds for only a few minutes are almost worse than no playgrounds at all."

—*S.S.*
DALY CITY, CALIFORNIA
4 1

KEEP THE TV OUT OF YOUR HOUSE. Never use the TV as a de facto babysitter while dinner is being made or whatever. Increased TV watching is proportional to increased behavioral issues. Kids create a richer imaginary life when you turn them toward books.

—*ANONYMOUS*
BETHESDA, MARYLAND
9 6

Blow bubbles in the bathtub. If you spill, it doesn't matter.

—*ELIZABETH*
FORT COLLINS, COLORADO

HIDE AND SEEK IS THE CLASSIC. That, and peek-a-boo with a blanket. Both my kids live for hide and seek. Kids love looking for you and screaming like crazy when they suddenly find you.

—*DAVID E. LISS*
PENNINGTON, NEW JERSEY
4 1

Please, never take a baby out to eat.

—*Anonymous*
Montclair, New Jersey

Lather yourself and your baby with sunscreen (careful near the eyes), plop on floppy hats, and go out and play! Sure, the housework needs to be done, but it can wait. Even if you're drained, a trip to the park will perk you up . . . and maybe even help your baby take a nice, long nap afterwards.

—*Graciela Sholander*
Fort Collins, Colorado
12 10

"We dressed our five kids alike when we traveled, so that if one got lost, we could point to the others and say, 'He looks just like him . . . only smaller.'"

—*Elaine Fantle Shimberg*
Tampa, Florida
41 40 38 37 32

I had my daughter help assemble an Adirondack chair with me when she was 14 months old. She handed me the screws and felt like she was helping. We painted a room together too. She made an absolute mess but she really felt like she was a part of it. Having her help allows me to get things done, and usually the mess cleans up easily.

—*Nancy*
Portland, Maine
2

THE MOMENT I TOOK MY SON OUTSIDE, whether it was snowing or sunny, he was happy as can be. I recommend that you get out as much as you can—nurse outside, attach the baby jumper to a tree, take a portable cradlette. I loved to put my son in a carrier on my back, put on my snow-shoes and go outside for a walk.

—JENNIFER TAYLOR ATANDA
ALEXANDRIA, VIRGINIA
2

Be prepared for anything. Always have an extra set of clothes, a camera for all those "firsts," snacks, diaper wipes, and a first aid kit.

—JESSICA
MILLIKEN,
COLORADO
2 3M

GO TO MUSEUMS WHEN THEY ARE INFANTS, because you won't be able to go later. Once they are toddlers, stick to the playground. Camping is great, but not until they are over one year old. The beach is great anytime. The beach makes the best all-around family vacation.

—JESSICA VAUGHAN
RANDOLPH, VERMONT
10 8 6 4

GO OUTSIDE AND PLAY! I think it's really important for mom and baby to get out and talk with other moms and kids and socialize. We live close to the park and we walk there every day. Sometimes we sit and watch the geese and ducks on the pond.

—SUZANNE NAYDUCH
FORT COLLINS, COLORADO
8M

KIDS LOVE TO SHARE YOUR interests with you, and you should make time to be with them, even if it's when you're performing household tasks. I built a swing set for my son. At age one year and nine months, he was my key helper.

—BILL
BOSTON, MASSACHUSETTS
-2

People think they need to entertain their kids constantly. Don't! I remember having babies and toddlers who were just so content to sit on a floor with a simple toy or a book or paper and crayons or even just some cardboard, and they would play for a long time. They learned how to use their imaginations and entertain themselves. Those are valuable skills.

—Matt W.
San Carlos, California
24 22 19

When my daughter was really little she liked watching birds, so we'd go to a local bookstore with a big window where we could watch them. They'd flap their wings and she'd giggle in hysterics.

—Tallie Fishburne
Minneapolis, Minnesota
14M

We bought a DVD player with an LCD screen for the car. We stick it on the back of the seat for the kids. It's great for road trips.

—Tami Meyers
Fort Collins, Colorado
11 7 4

Introduce your child to music right away. As a baby, my oldest child was colicky, so I got a CD player for her early on to soothe her. It helped a little, but the real benefit from that early exposure to music is that now she's a singer and a dancer; she absolutely loves music.

—Tina Smith
Fort Collins, Colorado
4 2

We thought it would be great to take our son to the zoo when he was six months old, but he was too young to be engaged or even interested. We stood in front of this elephant for 15 minutes, while he looked down at a patch of dirt on the ground.

—R.Q.
San Francisco, California
6M

CHILD'S PLAY

A SIMPLE RASPBERRY—OR BRONX CHEER, as it once was called—will make a child smile as easily (and much more cheaply) than any toy. Bouncing a baby on my knees, walking her under the bow of a leafing tree, exploring the cats' toes—it all delighted her more, much more, than some huge plastic thing that whirls and gongs and whizzes.

—Marion Roach
Troy, New York

OUR DAUGHTER THOUGHT IT WAS A RIOT WHEN I DROPPED a towel on her and covered her up after her bath. We would do this over and over, with her laughter cracking me up. It was totally ridiculous and so much fun.

—Nancy English
Portland, Maine

PLAY WITH YOUR BABY. It's important for you and the baby. It makes you both laugh and you can learn from the baby how to be more spontaneous and have more fun. Shake your head in a silly way, stick out your tongue, cross your eyes—babies really appreciate simple games like that.

—S.C.
Helotes, Texas
30

Go to Club Med. They have the best vacations if you have a baby.

—*L.C.*
PITTSBURGH, PENNSYLVANIA
6 5

DON'T FEEL LIKE YOU HAVE TO MOVE to the suburbs to raise kids. I love having urban kids. I don't have to drive much, which means a lot less hassle getting them in and out of the car. We just get in the stroller and off we go! And there is so much to do with them—museums with activities for kids, huge parks and playgrounds, and mommy groups. It keeps life more interesting for me as a stay-at-home mom, too!

—*RACHEL B.*
PHILADELPHIA, PENNSYLVANIA
3 2

"Even if you're totally against drugs, Benadryl for Children is a great emergency air travel trick. It'll have them sleep through the flight."

—*DIANA WILLIAMS*
MILL VALLEY, CALIFORNIA
-5 18M

DON'T "DUMB IT DOWN" FOR YOUR CHILDREN. My one-year-old son loves the music that my husband and I listen to—salsa and jazz—and when we're driving he loves the classic R&B radio station. Kiddie music does not appeal to him.

—*C.C.*
SAN FRANCISCO, CALIFORNIA
1

IT'S NEVER TOO EARLY TO SIGN up for exercise classes with your babies. At three months, children can start something like a "Music Together" program. My Mommy & Me class offers stretching and low-impact aerobics, using exercise bands. Classes organized through the city or community centers are great; they provide socialization before the kids begin pre-school—and, it's motivating to be with other mothers.

—*T.N.*
HUNTINGTON BEACH, CALIFORNIA
19M 3.5M

We've always carried the baby in a backpack instead of a stroller. It helped him stay connected, and the body warmth helped orient him.

—*NORA & BRIAN TRAINUM*
CHARLOTTE, NORTH CAROLINA
18

RIGHT FROM THE BEGINNING, OUR LITTLE GUY loved music and by 16 months he could identify all four Beatles! We listen to all kinds of music with him and get a kick out of how fast he'll say, "Not that one," after just a few notes. It's like "Name That Tune" with a toddler!

—*CHRISTINE BEIDEL*
RUTHERFORD, NEW JERSEY
11 2

WHEN MY HUSBAND AND I WERE PLANNING our vacation to Venice, Italy, we didn't prepare for traveling with a baby. We packed everything we would need for the baby, but Venice is not a stroller-friendly city—mostly because you need to take small boats to get around and strollers did not work well in the boats. To make it worse, I brought the big stroller because I thought that the baby would be more comfortable. He was more comfortable. But we were limited in what we could do and where we could go.

—*LORAINE BRANCATTO BOERSMA*
TOLEDO, OHIO
6 4

WHEN GOING ON A FAMILY VACATION, definitely get the kids loaded up with lots of activities—coloring and activity books, even a mini-walkman to listen to music. We play the alphabet game—you call out the letters on the road signs from "A" to "Z"—and other games like that.

—*K.J.*
ST. AUGUSTINE, FLORIDA
6 1

When we take car trips, the key is to listen to Sesame Street CDs on the ride. It calms and entertains my daughter and she doesn't scream the whole way.

—*RUSSELL LISSAU*
ARLINGTON HEIGHTS, ILLINOIS
2

MY BABY HATED BEING CONFINED to her carseat, and she would become so hysterical that I would have to pull over many times to get out and comfort her. I learned that when traveling a long distance, I should plan for someone to come with me to sit with her and distract her. Lots of snacks and toys help too.

—*PAULA FOX*
GORHAM, MAINE
2

WE'VE TAKEN OUR THREE-YEAR-OLD on at least 20 round trip flights, and our one-year-old on about eight. We've hardly found it worthwhile to buy an extra seat for the kid, since they hardly napped and won't stay there when they can be on your lap or eating peanuts off the floor. Also, you can just bring a car seat on the plane and hope you get lucky with an extra seat; even if there are not continuous seats, people will be more than happy to get out of your way so they don't end up next to a baby. For entertainment, kids are absolutely fascinated by the barf bag, flight safety card, and plastic cups (ask for an extra one). If that fails to amuse them, try bribery—our three-year-old gets M&Ms if she's good on the flight.

—*MARK KAPLAN*
FOSTER CITY, CALIFORNIA
3 1

IT'S EASIER TO TAKE A ROAD TRIP WITH A BABY if you put them in the car at their bedtime and drive through the night. That way, he or she can sleep during the ride and you can concentrate on driving. We did this on a trip from Philadelphia to Iowa and it worked perfectly. The next time, we drove during the day and it was a rough ride.

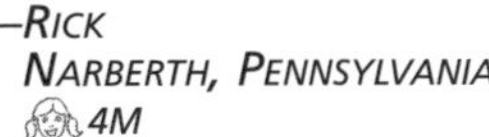

—RICK
NARBERTH, PENNSYLVANIA
4M

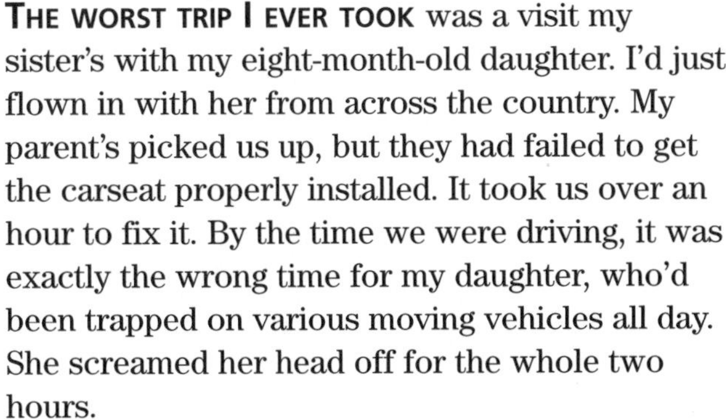

THE WORST TRIP I EVER TOOK was a visit my sister's with my eight-month-old daughter. I'd just flown in with her from across the country. My parent's picked us up, but they had failed to get the carseat properly installed. It took us over an hour to fix it. By the time we were driving, it was exactly the wrong time for my daughter, who'd been trapped on various moving vehicles all day. She screamed her head off for the whole two hours.

—JENNY W.
NEW YORK, NEW YORK
4

DON'T MAKE THE MISTAKE OF TRAVELING through the night when your baby sleeps. If you do, when the day comes, you won't have gotten any sleep but your baby will be wide awake and ready to go. I've seen lots of people try this, and they just get frustrated. Instead, we leave around six a.m. and stop driving for the day around four p.m. It works very well.

—STACY MCHARGUE
SAN ANTONIO, TEXAS
12 11

SING IT LOUD

Sing to your baby. Babies love music. Singing is very soothing. I have to do that a lot as a nanny with the twins I take care of. If they're both crying, I can't take care of both of them at the same time. When I'm trying to get them ready to eat, they're usually both crying as I'm mixing up their cereal. They start listening to me singing and they forget their troubles a little bit.

If they're fussing while I'm feeding them and having a hard time accepting the food, the singing always seems to work. The song they like at the moment is, "The Wheels On the Bus."

I try to be animated when I sing. I dance around the room a little bit. The motion gets their attention. They stop dead in their tracks like they've seen a ghost and stare at me. Then, they smile because they're like, "Oh, I kind of like this song." If there's an older child, have him or her help. I'll say, "Do a dance for the baby."

—*Debbie L.*
Camillus, New York
12

Our son often falls asleep in the car, so it makes traveling by car easy. The down side of that, though, is that he sleeps the whole drive and the moment we get to our destination he's ready to go, whether we are or not!

—Robyn
Biglerville, Pennsylvania
1

• • • • • • • •

Air travel with a baby is a breeze. Strollers can be checked at the gate and when the plane lands, you get it right back. Also, a lot of car rental places let you check out car seats so you don't have to bring your own. When we travel we look for places that rent child-friendly equipment, like beach joggers. Usually you can get what you need delivered right to your door.

—Stephanie
Windsor, Colorado
2 7M

• • • • • • • •

Remember that a baby has as much right to be on a plane as that cranky, child-less business traveler who thinks the world revolves around him or her. Sure, the baby disrupts the flight with screaming, fussing, uncontainable laughter, playing patty cake with the head of the person in front of them. But the cranky, child-less business traveler disrupts the flight with rude stares, loud and selfish complaints, and bad karma. And they won't even hold your kid for one minute while you clean up the puke on the floor. Personally, I don't think cranky, child-less business travelers should be allowed on planes. They can't handle the tight, stressful quarters for such long periods of time. But unless the airlines change the rules, I won't make an issue out of it.

—JWAIII
Atlanta, Georgia
5 2

Don't be afraid to take the baby to restaurants in the very beginning. When they are infants there's a great window of opportunity to get out without much fuss.

—Russ Cox
Portland, Maine
-5 1

BEFORE YOU TRAVEL WITH A BABY on a bus, train, or plane, take a six-foot-long piece of parachute cord (or other strong cord) and tie four or five toys to it. This way, when your kid tries to throw the toys, they don't go far, and you won't spend half of your journey crawling on the floor trying to retrieve them. (Of course, this is not for unattended play, but it should be perfectly safe while you're sitting right beside your baby.)

—JEAN NICK
KINTNERSVILLE, PENNSYLVANIA
16 14

Never be afraid to do things with your family. Buy backpacks and a bike trailer—you can take your kids with you anywhere.

—NICOLE DAVIS
RACHO CORDOVA
10 5 2

I JUST TRAVELED WITH MY 15-MONTH-OLD SON from Tanzania without my wife because we couldn't get on the same flight. The plane ride was 17 hours and it was the first time I had spent more than one or two hours alone with him. Changing diapers on the plane was difficult and there were times when my son was crying and I did not know what to do. But I cherished the experience.

—M.Z. NAAB
ARLINGTON, VIRGINIA
15M

IT IS AN UNMITIGATED PAIN, BUT ALSO WORTH IT to lug car seats onto the airplane for trips of any considerable distance. We did it and while we could have lived without the angry stares from other passengers—especially when a flight attendant had to order the pilot to stop the plane as we taxied toward takeoff so one of the car seats could be moved to the aisle seat—it allowed both our children to snooze peacefully almost the entire two-plus hour flight. Plus, we knew the kids were safe when we put them in our rental car.

—KEITH REGAN
GRAFTON, MASSACHUSETTS
5 3

IF YOU'RE FLYING WITH AN INFANT, make sure the baby is drinking from a bottle on the way up and on the way down. This keeps the ears open and the child from crying due to ears hurting from the change in altitude. And a change of clothes is a must, along with a travel stroller that allows you to wheel the baby right up to your seat.

—*JANE COVNER*
SHERMAN OAKS, CALIFORNIA
18

I swap toys with other parents whose kids have outgrown them. It saves money, and once my kids have outgrown the toys, I pass them to the next mom down the line.

—*ANONYMOUS*
NEW TRIPOLI, PENNSYLVANIA
3 14W

NEVER TRAVEL ON AN AIRPLANE with a baby. You've got to take the car seat and when they are awake, everyone's awake. We took my son at 10 months. He was starting to walk, so he wanted to be able to move around and crawl but couldn't. And you know, there is soooooo much space on an airplane to change a diaper.

—*WESLEY ANDERSON*
SAN ANTONIO, TEXAS
2

THE FIRST TIME WE FLEW WITH OUR DAUGHTER, she stayed on my wife's lap. The woman who sat in front of them was wearing a big black hat with tons of these little colorful pins all over it. The pins had little cars, little teddy bears, little toys, hanging off them. Our daughter's eyes lit up. She lunged for the hat as I held her back with all I had in me. The rest of the flight (we hadn't even taxied down the runway yet) is gone from my memory.

—*DAVID LISS*
PENNINGTON, NEW JERSEY
4 1

Traveling with a baby is easy. They mostly sleep on plane and car trips because there is nothing else to do.

—*Anonymous*
Golden, Colorado
15M

When you're on a plane you don't care if your kids are going crazy. But when it's another kid, you're like, "Man, can someone shut that kid up?"

—*Eddie Finkelstein*
Chappaqua, New York
16 14 9

I always talked to the babies and babbled away at them about whatever I was doing or thinking. I think that communication is really important, even when the baby can't understand.

—*Brette Sember*
Clarence, New York
12 6

I love trying to make my daughter laugh and trying to entertain her. Of course it usually only lasts about 15 minutes before she loses interest.

—*John D. Calley*
Alexandria, Virginia
4M

12

An Apple a Day: Health and Growth Issues

Bumps and bruises. Coughs and sniffles. As your child grows, so does your concern for their health and safety. Not sure you have what it takes to get your baby through in one piece? Cover your outlets, lock your cabinets, get out the baby aspirin and keep reading for advice on everything from worst case scenarios to good-for-you foods.

BABIES CAN FIND WAYS TO GET THEMSELVES into mischief, so you have to think ahead. If there is something that you are not sure is secure, then secure it.

—*MARIA*
EAST PALESTINE, OHIO
18 16 12

YOU DON'T KNOW WHAT IT MEANS TO BE A PARENT UNTIL YOUR BABY STARTS TO CRAWL.

—*JWAIII*
ATLANTA, GEORGIA
5 2

ENJOY EACH UNIQUE STAGE of your child's development. Some people say, "I can't wait until he gets to walking or talking." As you keep wishing, they'll grow faster and you'll miss things.

—*KEN BECKERING*
SYRACUSE, NEW YORK
5 3

Sunscreen stick is really handy. It's like Chapstick; it's easy to apply.

—*J. MCNALLY*
LOVELAND, COLORADO
9 7 16M

WE ALWAYS WANTED THREE KIDS, but now that we've got them we realize, "Oh no! We're outnumbered!" And they're all at an age that's totally unpredictable. If we're watching one of the younger ones, we turn around and find out the oldest one was drawing on a wall. If we take the older two, the youngest just crawls towards the most dangerous object around. And Lord knows we're not foolish enough to leave the one in his terrible twos unmanned. Help!

—*J.R.*
CHICAGO, ILLINOIS
4 2 1

I HAD ALWAYS LEFT MY BABY ON THE SOFA, with a soft ottoman pulled in tight, and she was always safe and fine. One day, before I even knew she could really crawl, I was in another room and I heard this thump. I ran in and of course she had scooted herself off the edge of the sofa. Luckily, she wasn't really hurt, but I finally believed it when people warned me not to leave a child on sofas, chairs, or other "high" places!

—*K. JONES*
PHILADELPHIA, PENNSYLVANIA
14 10 6

GET THE LEAD OUT

I thought I had my whole house baby-proofed when my son was just starting to walk. And then I read this article in a magazine about a family whose two children got severe lead poisoning when they renovated their gorgeous Victorian home. So I learned that lead isn't just a problem for people living in cities. Apparently all old houses have lead in them and the lead chips from paint aren't necessarily the biggest problem; the lead dust from original windows or cabinets that are opened and closed is a problem, too, especially when you renovate, because you cut through layers of paint and the lead dust flies everywhere, landing on toys, etc. This lead arrests brain development and can cause aggression and hyperactivity and many other problems.

We bought a house from the 1920s and it has all of its original windowsills and cabinets. I decided to ask my pediatrician to test my son. My doctor actually said that we didn't "fit the demographic" and didn't recommend testing. I did more research, switched doctors and tested him again and he did have a low level of lead poisoning—enough to worry us. Thank God I pushed it with my doctor. Anyone living in an old house who is renovating can be exposed. My advice is to not renovate while you have a baby in the house (if your house is over 35 years old) and if you do, hire a lead specialist to work with your contractor to seal off the areas tightly and to test afterwards.

—M. Soelberg
Los Angeles, California
3

OUR 14-MONTH-OLD DAUGHTER is a little ball of energy. Once, we were walking out of a Vietnamese restaurant and she went dashing out the door, nearly into traffic. As much as you hear people say it, it holds so true: You have to watch your children at all times. You never know when your child will dart off and find a bottle of Crystal Drano.

—*KERRY ROME*
HERMOSA BEACH, CALIFORNIA
14M

"By the end of the first year, you'll know every type of antibiotic and cough syrup that's out there."

—*JENNIFER FELTON*
BATON ROUGE, LOUISIANA
2 1

A VERY HELPFUL PHRASE TO TEACH small kids is "come here." This works great if you need to distract your kids to stop them from fighting. It can also be a lifesaver if they're doing something dangerous. It's a very positive intervention. Rather than yelling at them, you're simply telling them to "come here."

—*TORI DENNIS*
IRON CITY, TENNESSEE
8 6 5

KEEP THE TOLL-FREE POISON emergency hotline number (1-800-222-1222) near the phone and call immediately if you suspect your child has been in contact with a poison. Even in a "baby-proofed" home, bad things can happen and parents should have no fear of being judged for "allowing" their child to touch/taste/breathe a poison. Calls to a poison center are handled by nurses, pharmacists and doctors and are completely confidential.

—*CHRIS FALK*
CHEVY CHASE, MARYLAND
4 1.5

INFANT INFO

Having a dog around the house during your baby's first year of life may lead to a reduction in allergies as he or she grows older.

AVOID PERMANENT MARKERS LIKE THE PLAGUE. When my daughter was around two, we had just had the house painted and she saw the electrical outlet in the wall, which had no plastic plugs. She saw the two little vertical lines with the little hole and thought it looked like a bunny rabbit's face. With a permanent marker, she drew the ears of the bunny to go with it. It wasn't dangerous, but it was maddening and hilarious.

—*NAOMI NEMTZOW*
BROOKLYN, NEW YORK
22 -15

BEFORE THE CHILDREN CAN CRAWL, remove all CDs from the premises. Every single one of them is a meal waiting to be eaten, as well as a little book (you know, the liner notes) waiting to be ripped or chewed to shreds. I'm not saying I have to replace my entire CD collection. Just about a third of it.

—*DAVID E. LISS*
PENNINGTON, NEW JERSEY
4 1

USE A SPECIAL WORD TO GET THEIR ATTENTION quickly. Instead of always saying "No," or "Don't do that," we have two special words that we use for situations when we want our daughter to stop quickly. The first word is "danger." We say "Danger!" to prevent her from getting hurt, as in "Don't run into the street," or "Don't climb on top of the cabinets." The second word is "ugly." We use this one to stop behavior that's not nice, like hitting or pushing.

—SHARI LONG, CNM (MIDWIFE)
CHEYENNE, WYOMING
21 19 12 2

Don't panic when your child is sick. When my son got croup, I didn't know it was a fairly simple thing. It sounded so scary, but it wasn't so bad.

—JULIE
FORT COLLINS, COLORADO
8

WHEN MY FIRST CHILD TURNED TWO, I introduced him to the world of chocolate. I gave him one small piece, but he wanted more. So I thought, "Why not?" and gave him a couple more pieces. I inadvertently left the chocolate bar in a place too accessible to his little hands. Within a second of me turning my head, he had stuffed an entire bar into his mouth, wrapping and all. I was terrified that he was going to start choking, but he wolfed down everything and sat there with a look on his face that said, "More." Of course, later that day he was sick as a dog.

—BILLIE
NEW YORK, NEW YORK
5 18M

GET OVER THE IDEA THAT BY NOT HANDING your baby to other people you'll protect them from diseases. Just start letting them go when they're young or you'll end up causing serious damage. You've got to get them out there, starting when they're three days old.

—ANONYMOUS
BETHESDA, MARYLAND
9 6

HAVE AN EMERGENCY NUMBER HANDY. One night, my nine-month-old daughter started choking on bread. I was terrified. I didn't know what to do to stop the choking so I called the emergency number. The operator told me that, since she was not turning blue, she was still getting air. They instructed me to give her some water to wash it down. It worked! Thankfully, they stayed on the phone with me until she stopped choking and was breathing normally. The whole event lasted only about two minutes, but it was the scariest two minutes of my life.

—*F.T.L.*
METZ, FRANCE
5 3

"Fathers should not try to hold a sick baby above their shoulders. And mothers should not laugh when he gets puked on."

—*D.R.*
SYRACUSE, NEW YORK
8 4 16M

DON'T BE AFRAID TO CALL THE doctor if you think there is a problem, even a minor one. Most first-time parents feel that people will think they are overreacting if they call for help every time the baby sneezes, but I've always said I'd rather be safe than sorry.

—*JIM R.*
NEGLEY, OHIO
15

BABY FOOD . . . MMM, GOOD

MAKE YOUR OWN BABY FOOD! I know that many people feel they don't have the time—especially with everything else you're doing every day for baby. I was reluctant, too. But it is so easy and quick. And it's much healthier than buying it. I made my own baby food without using a blender. Just ask your friends if you can have their Gerber jars so you can put your own food in them.

—NANCY
BRUSSELS, BELGIUM

• • • • • • • •

FOOD IS TRICKY. Sometimes I go to bed at the end of the day and I wonder, "What did my daughter eat that's healthy?" I just keep offering her good foods, but I don't make special meals just for her. She has to learn to eat what the rest of us eat.

—CHERI
FORT COLLINS, COLORADO
1

• • • • • • • •

HAVE YOU EVER TASTED STORE-BOUGHT BABY FOOD? It's terrible. When my daughter was a baby, I vowed that I wouldn't feed her anything that I wouldn't eat myself. Instead, I pureed some of the food that my husband and I were eating and fed it to her. It worked great, especially with carrots, peas, and sweet potatoes. I'd freeze any leftover puree in ice cube trays. Then if I needed a quick meal for her, it was simple to defrost a cube or two in the microwave for a few seconds.

—CAROL GILMORE
EASTON, PENNSYLVANIA
6

• • • • • • • •

LITTLE KNOWN FACT: Baby food—particularly the peaches, pears or plums—is really quite tasty.

—GEORGINA
ATLANTA, GEORGIA
35

I REFUSED TO BUY BABY FOOD. Instead, I ground up my own fresh carrots and green beans, I made homemade yogurt and granola, and I fed my babies breast milk. The natural method saved me money and worked wonders for their health. To this day, they don't get ear infections, and they're lean and trim with tons of energy.

—S.H.
NEW LENOX, ILLINOIS
25 17 15

• • • • • • • •

DON'T BE AFRAID TO FEED KIDS A VARIETY OF "ADULT" FOODS, not just the same old mashed banana baby foods. I had a little blender set up in the kitchen. I would just take whatever we were eating, unless it was something spicy, and blend it up for the babies. They ate well and all grew up to be great eaters.

—LORI T.
CHARLESTON, SOUTH CAROLINA
36 34 31 26

• • • • • • • •

WHEN I WAS IN FRANCE, I NOTICED THE BABIES there ate all sorts of "real" food—not just the usual chicken nuggets and PBJs I was used to seeing kids eat. Somebody there told me the secret was to give babies regular adult food, just pureed. So, when we had our own babies, we gave them pureed "real" food as soon as possible. I have friends who say their kids just wanted milk or rice cereal, but my babies ate lasagna, garlicky pasta salad, stewed veggies, strong cheeses, and even slightly spicy foods. And now they just happily eat whatever we eat!

—J.W.
ROCHESTER, NEW YORK
-13

WITH MY SONS, I WAS TOO PROTECTIVE. I was always shielding them, trying to keep them close. I have a totally different perspective with my fourth child, who's my only daughter. I expose her to many different situations and people, and as a result she's happy, outgoing, and joyful.

—*SHARI LONG, CNM (MIDWIFE)*
CHEYENNE, WYOMING
21 19 12 2

IF YOUR CHILD HAS AN EAR INFECTION, don't call the doctor. Take him to a homeopath or naturopath. My son used to have ear infections every month. The doctor gave him antibiotics, which cleared up the infection. But it kept returning. When I finally took him to a homeopath, she gave him herbs for the pain and natural substances for the infection. It cleared up within a day. Then she tested him for allergies. We discovered that he was allergic to soy milk and cow's milk. Once we started giving him rice milk, he stopped having ear infections, his skin became very clear, and he felt better.

—*F.T.L.*
METZ, FRANCE
5 3

TO KEEP MY CABINET CONTENTS INTACT and still keep my kids safe, I chose the cabinet farthest away from the refrigerator and stove and dedicated it to their stuff. I put all of their dishes and sippy cups in it. My daughter and my son both know that it is their cabinet. Then, when they try to go into other cabinets, I firmly say, "No, that's Mommy's." It's really amazing how well this simple technique works.

—*PAULA*
NORTHAMPTON, PENNSYLVANIA
3 1

MAKE SURE YOU BABY-PROOF THE HOUSE before your kid can crawl, which can happen very suddenly. I left my daughter in her normal play area well before she could crawl and went in the other room for 30 seconds to get socks. When I came back, she had rolled all the way over to a very heavy, breakable, tippy pot we had on the floor. Luckily, both the pot and baby were fine, but another five seconds and it would have been a different story.

—S. Coleman
New York, New York
8M

• • • • • • • •

FOR DIARRHEA, I HAVE THE BEST CURE: charcoal! No, don't head over to the barbecue grill. Go to a health food store or pharmacist and buy charcoal tablets. This is a very common and natural cure used in Sweden. For my infant son, I grind the tablets into his food. It helps to absorb water so the diarrhea is cured quickly and gently. Important point: Don't give too much because it can cause constipation.

—J.K.
Belgium/Sweden
3

• • • • • • • •

BRONCHITIS CAN BE EASILY CURED! My son constantly gets attacks of bronchitis after a cold. The doctors gave him antibiotics, which helped, but also gave him diarrhea. Now, I place a steamer in his room. Sometimes, I put a drop of eucalyptus in the steamer, but often plain water is enough. The steam loosens the phlegm so he can cough it up more easily. Within a day or two, the bronchitis is all gone—without using antibiotics!

—Beatrice
Miami, Florida

Introduce textured foods as soon as you can, like Cheerios, or soft flaky salmon, or juicy summer fruits. This will prevent them from being picky eaters.

—Daniela
Corte Madera, California
5 3

EARLY ON I REALIZED THAT THE ISSUE of clothing was a small battle, not one I was going to engage in. My daughter dislikes any bows, frills, epaulets. She likes sleek, simple things, despises dresses and has no patience for any patterns. And who cares? This is the small stuff. I choose which issues to battle over, and this in not one of them.

—Marion Roach
Troy, New York

ONE TIME, MY EIGHT-MONTH-OLD SON hit his head four times in one day. The first time, he crawled over my legs and fell on his head. Later, he tumbled out of his crib (we didn't even know he could climb!). The third time, he looked up and hit his head on the bars. The fourth, I was carrying him and dropped something, and when I went to pick it up, I hit his head on the side mirror of my car. I called the doctor's office and I was certain they would call child protective services. But they didn't, and he was fine.

—Anonymous
San Antonio, Texas
3 1 7M

WHEN YOU SCREW UP, don't get racked with guilt. We all do it. I felt so bad when my baby burned herself on a hot pan I'd left out. When I told people what happened, every parent had a similar story—dropping a kid, dropping something on a kid, burning a kid, forgetting a kid somewhere. People make mistakes. If the baby doesn't come out of the experience with any major injuries, just thank your lucky stars and move on with your life.

—Susan
Chicago, Illinois
4 1

WHEN MY SON WAS A YEAR AND A HALF OLD, he developed a fever and started acting unusually cranky, so we just assumed he was teething. One day, I went to pick him up at preschool and noticed his ear was incredibly hot and oozing yellow puss. Panicked, I rushed him to the doctor and found out his eardrum had burst while he was sleeping. The symptoms I had attributed to teething actually indicated the early stages of an ear infection, too. I wish I would have known this earlier.

—*CHERI HURD*
LITTLETON, COLORADO
26 23 21 14

• • • • • • • •

PARENTS WHO HAVE KIDS WITH CHRONIC EAR infections should at least look into the option of ear tubes. Our son had ear infections constantly, starting from about nine months old. We kept bringing him in to the doctor, who'd prescribe us antibiotics, and it would go away for a few weeks. Then it would come back and we'd do it all over again. I really hated giving him so many antibiotics. If I knew then what I know now, I think I would have had them do the surgery to put longer tubes in his ears. I realize the doctors do everything they can to avoid surgery, but I think that taking too many antibiotics is bad for the baby. And the infections were really painful.

—*JULIE*
SAN FRANCISCO, CALIFORNIA
13

MY HUSBAND WAS PLAYING with our daughter, lifting her up and swinging her around. They were laughing when we heard a pop. Our daughter's elbow had popped out of the joint! Because children have such flexible joints, it is easy for this to occur. She was in a lot of pain, but the doctor quickly popped it back into the joint. He advised us to be careful with young children and avoid swinging even during playtime.

—P.
PORTLAND, OREGON

WHEN MY KIDS GOT TO THE POINT where they wanted to dress themselves, I would try to coordinate everything—shirt, pants, socks, hair bow. But inevitably they'd want to wear their favorite socks or "best shirt" and it usually didn't match anything they had on. One day, my friend told me that if they're doing it themselves, then just deal with it. It may not be perfect, but at least you didn't have to do it. Even if nothing matches, who cares? They're proud that they've done something for themselves. That's all that really matters.

—J.K.
CLIFTON SPRINGS, NEW YORK
11 8

I WAS LUCKY. MY SISTER-IN-LAW had six kids, plus the people at my church were so tickled when I had twin girls that I didn't have to actually buy clothes until they were a 2T. Then, I basically hit Goodwill Stores or ReUzIt Shops. I still do, even for my oldest.

—JEANNE ECKMAN
LANCASTER, PENNSYLVANIA
11 - 5

WHEN MY SON WAS AROUND SIX WEEKS OLD, he had acid reflux and preferred to be upright as much as possible. At the time he would only sleep about a half hour at a time on his back. Even at night, I was lucky to get an hour and a half out of him. I was told to elevate one end of his crib to help him sleep. This didn't work at all, he simply slid down to one end of the crib. I decided to put my son in his infant car seat and place it in the crib. It worked like a charm!

—*SHEENA KROCK*
KUNKLETOWN, PENNSYLVANIA
14M

HAND-ME-DOWNS ARE OK FOR BABIES if the clothes are in good shape. They really won't know the difference. When they're crawling what's most important is to get sturdy clothes. And, they just need to be clean. When they're teething, it's a good idea to have babies wear a bib. Otherwise, their shirts get wet and worn when they chew on them.

—*PAM BOEA*
SYRACUSE, NEW YORK
19 17 -15 12

I ALWAYS LOVED TO SEW AND THOUGHT I'd sew all these adorable little baby clothes. But don't count on it—once you've got the baby, you'll barely have the time! Plus, baby clothes are not that expensive nowadays, unless you get the fancy stuff, and it probably costs more to buy the fabric than to just buy discount baby clothes.

—*JILL H.*
NEW YORK, NEW YORK
14 12

CLOTHES FOR BABY

EBAY! I LOVE EBAY! I have bought a lot of my son's clothing from eBay and saved a ton! You can get brand new clothing with the tags still attached for next to nothing. You can also get clothing inexpensively by buying it out of season.

—Erin Callahan
Kershaw, South Carolina
2

• • • • • • • •

THERE IS A WEB SITE CALLED FREECYCLE.ORG where people are giving away things for free. All you have to do is go pick it up! This is a great way to get free baby clothes, and get rid of ones your child has outgrown.

—Jessica L. Delaney
Johnstown, Colorado
4 2

• • • • • • • •

THE BEST PLACE TO GET BOTH MATERNITY CLOTHES and baby clothes are consignment stores. There are good selections and the prices are very reasonable. When you're done with the clothes you can just bring them back to the store for credit and exchange them for other "new" items.

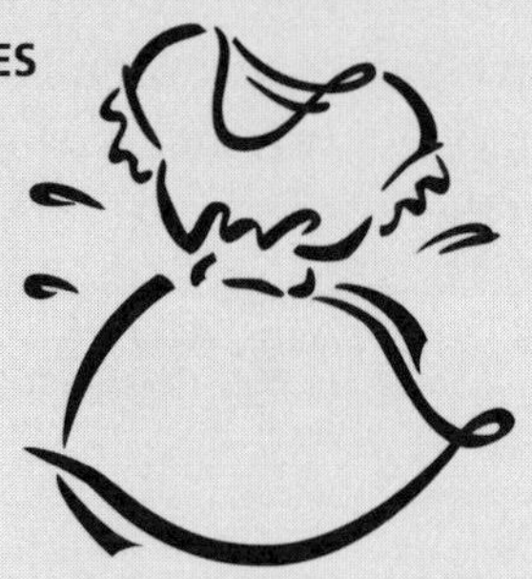

—Anonymous
Alameda, California
7M

• • • • • • • •

DON'T BUY THOSE TEENY-TINY LITTLE SHOES. They may be cute as a button, but they're not good for helping your baby learn to walk. Babies should not wear shoes until they're walking outdoors.

—Rachel B.
Philadelphia, Pennsylvania
3 2

YOU CAN SAVE A LOT OF MONEY by passing around baby clothes, either as hand-me-downs or temporary loaners, while you wait for the next kid to come along. I've done this with my friends, and I've barely had to buy any clothes.

—*KATRINA CURRIER*
SAN FRANCISCO, CALIFORNIA
17M

• • • • • • • •

NEVER BUY CLOTHES THAT YOU THINK YOUR BABY will "fit into later" because that never works. Buy for what size they are now. I still have baby clothes with tags on them that I was waiting to put my daughters in. They are teenagers now.

—*KAREN*
DEER PARK, ILLINOIS
13 11 2

• • • • • • • •

HAVE A WIDE VARIETY OF SIZES AVAILABLE for the baby. My first weighed 11½ pounds and was into three-month size immediately and then soon into six-month size. My second, however, was eight pounds, 14 ounces and wore newborn clothes.

—*BRETTE SEMBER*
CLARENCE, NEW YORK
12 6

DON'T TAKE THE SIZE TAGS ON BABY CLOTHES too literally. My daughter is 10 months old and wears some sweaters that say "newborn, 0-3 months," some pants that say "3-6 months," some sleepers that say "6-9" or "6-12 months," and a hat that says "12-18 months." Sweaters, especially, seem to run big for some reason.

—K.T.
BURLINGTON, VERMONT
5 4 1

BUY AHEAD. GET CLOTHES AT the end of a season for the size your kid will be next year. You'll save tons of money!

—J.D.
BALTIMORE, MARYLAND
15 3

AFTER MY GRANDSON STARTED TO CRAWL, my daughter literally crawled all around the house so she could see from a baby's perspective what he could get into, hurt himself with, etc.

—NOLA SMITH
TAMPA, FLORIDA
41 35

Your Little Genius: Walking, Talking, and Learning

So you turned around to grab the laundry, and when you looked back your kid was walking and talking. It happens so fast! What's next, college? Don't laugh—it's not that far away. In the (short) meantime, you'll want to start teaching your child and his or her super-absorbent brain. What's the best way to nurture your little Einstein? Read on.

KIDS WALK WHEN THEY ARE READY, talk when they are ready, potty train when they are ready, etc. We don't need to worry about these developmental milestones, compare our kids to others, or try to speed these things along. That just makes the parents nuts and makes the child feel inadequate.

—*ANONYMOUS*
SAN ANTONIO, TEXAS
9 6

DON'T BE IN SUCH A RUSH TO TRAIN YOUR BABY TO WALK. THEY'RE A HANDFUL AFTER THAT!

—*J.W.*
ROCHESTER, NEW YORK
- 13

My daughter took her first steps when we were on vacation in Bar Harbor, Maine, and I'm pretty sure I'll never forget every last detail.

—*Keith Regan*
Grafton, Massachusetts
5 3

I knew my son was special when the nurse said that he was the only baby in the hospital nursery who watched her as she moved around the room; she said it was unnerving to be observed by so young a baby.

—*Janny Tang*
Santa Cruz, California
31

Read all the baby books with a grain of salt and with the knowledge that your child probably isn't going to fit into whatever model they are espousing. I've noticed they are usually a little more advanced than your baby should or will be at a particular time. They start talking about sleep training at three months, when it's close to impossible before six months; one book mentions your child saying "no" all the time at 12 months, when most babies haven't spoken their first words yet; they speak of reading your child a bedtime story, but this is hard to do before they are about 10 months old, because they just want to eat the book.

—*Barbara McGlamery*

Don't put your baby on a scale—like, all one-year-olds need to be walking. My nephew was tested for being slow because he hadn't started walking at 12 months. He was just fine; he walked at 13 months. He just didn't have a reason to do it yet. The other kids were bringing him stuff.

—*Catherine Grinda*
Atascosa, Texas
- - 16M

MY DAUGHTER WAS ON THE LATE SIDE for walking; at 15 months she still just didn't seem to care about it. Then one day, that all changed. I had ordered her a pair of sneakers on eBay, and when she saw them she immediately grabbed the shoe laces, stood up and started jiggling them up and down. Eureka! The advantage of standing upright! Hands are available! She took several steps just while playing with the shoes, and she never looked back.

—CATHY C.
BIDDEFORD, MAINE
4

• • • • • • • • •

WE READ PICTURE BOOKS TO MY GRANDSON all the time. I would take my finger and trace the letters. I would use my finger to count the butterflies on the page. It helps your baby focus on the page.

—J.K. DAPRATO
VANCOUVER, WASHINGTON
36 33

• • • • • • • • •

WHEN YOUR CHILD IS LEARNING TO WALK, cheer him on. Those first steps are a very magical moment, for both you and your baby. When they take those first steps, they get as excited as you do—they clap and smile. We encourage them through positive reinforcement.

—ALANA SIMMS
FORT COLLINS, COLORADO
4 1

TO TEACH YOUR BABY TO WALK, sit with them on the floor and give them encouragement. Also, do leg exercises—it will make them strong. You can stand them on your legs and put them on their backs. Then you grab their ankles and push their knees to their tummy. I did this, and my daughter walked at 10 months and my son at 11 months.

—*GLORIA A. SOLIS*
SAN ANTONIO, TEXAS
15 12

• • • • • • • •

WHEN MY DAUGHTER STARTED to learn to walk, we bought this huge pad that wrapped around our coffee table in the living room. It was designed to cover the corners, but it was always sagging in one area, and it was probably the ugliest thing we could put in our living room. And it was all for naught—one day my daughter was standing at a nearby chair and decided to make the trek to the table, but halfway there she stumbled. Of course, the one part of the table that wasn't covered by that sagging, ugly pad was the corner where she fell and met it with her forehead. She got a nice goose egg from that, but she was OK. And the pad was immediately removed and tossed in the trash.

—*JWAIII*
ATLANTA, GEORGIA
5 2

INFANT INFO

Some parents tend to be too overbearing on their newborns. Excessive parental concern may impede a child's language development.

WHEN BABY FALLS ...

IT'S HARD TO WATCH YOUR CHILD FALLING AND HITTING HER HEAD when she's little, but kids' bodies are made for that. When they learn to walk, they fall. You've got to watch out for sharp corners far more than just a simple "thud" onto the ground.

—N. CLARK
HOUSTON, TEXAS
15

• • • • • • • •

WHEN OUR KIDS WOULD FALL DOWN, if we rushed over and made a fuss, they would cry. If we just nonchalantly helped them up or even looked away, they usually just sat up and tried again. Save your pity and fussing for the really big falls.

—SEAN H.
NEW YORK, NEW YORK
14 12

• • • • • • • •

MY NATURAL REACTION WAS TO RUN OVER, pick up my daughter when she fell and ask her, "Are you OK?" Like a switch being thrown, she'd start crying. One time I saw her fall. She couldn't see me in the other room. I stood there to see what she was going to do. She got up like nothing happened. So after that, I'd still be concerned when she fell. But if I saw her get up and start looking around for me, I wouldn't acknowledge that she fell. Half the time—if not more than that—she wouldn't cry.

—JOHN D'EREDITA
SYRACUSE, NEW YORK
19 12

DON'T WORRY SO MUCH about what other people consider "normal." My son didn't walk till he was nearly two and everybody kept telling me it wasn't normal and that I should be worried. When he finally did take his first step, he pretty much got up and walked across the room. He ended up being a track star.

—*BONNIE DULFON*
BOSTON, MASSACHUSETTS
42 41 36

"Don't use baby talk. You're teaching your child how to talk, modeling how words are supposed to sound. If you speak in a sing-song fashion, that's how your child will learn to speak."

—*SARA*
ST. LOUIS PARK, MINNESOTA
4 2

WHEN YOUR BABY IS OLD ENOUGH to keep his or her head up, read to them. I propped them on my lap and started reading books. That increased their ability to speak and understand language. When they were two, they were already speaking in phrases.

—*JOBETH MCLEOD*
SAN ANTONIO, TEXAS
26 18

MY GRANDSON STARTED WALKING at about a year and a half. He had been crawling for some time and pulling himself up, but not walking. Then one day while he was with my daughter at a library, he just stood up and walked away, as if he had been doing it for weeks. I told my daughter he was probably practicing when no one was watching!

—John R. Bright
Allentown, Pennsylvania
33 31

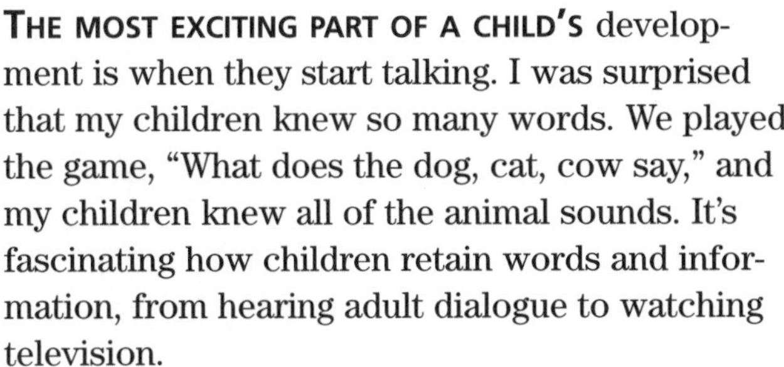

THE MOST EXCITING PART OF A CHILD'S development is when they start talking. I was surprised that my children knew so many words. We played the game, "What does the dog, cat, cow say," and my children knew all of the animal sounds. It's fascinating how children retain words and information, from hearing adult dialogue to watching television.

—Nary Ba
Antioch, California
3 2

TALK TO YOUR BABY AND TELL HER what you're doing. That's what I do: "Hi Emily, I'm going to pick you up now." Or, "Emily, Mommy's going to bathe you now." It may seem very simple, but somehow it seems she's beginning to anticipate actions based on my tone or my sentence. There's recognition.

—M.B.
New York, New York
7M

Teaching a baby sign language helps them communicate earlier, and it won't hurt their regular language development.

—K.C.
San Francisco, California
2

PROVIDE YOUR CHILD WITH PEERS to learn from. With my brother's triplets, each one watches everything the others do. Once one started crawling, the others watched with amazement. Within a month, they were all crawling.

—*CATHERINE GRINDA*
ATASCOSA, TEXAS
16M

Sing to your baby. I exposed my children to all kinds of music. Now when they hear old songs they think they've never heard before they still know all the words.

—*JOBETH MCLEOD*
SAN ANTONIO, TEXAS
26 18

READING TO CHILDREN IS SO IMPORTANT. My two older girls were toddlers when my third daughter was a baby, so I read to them every time I nursed the baby. That became our routine. We had an overstuffed rocking chair, and while I sat there, each one would sit on an arm of the chair. As I rocked the baby and read, they were being rocked, too. It was wonderful.

—*MARY LOBUE*
LAS VEGAS, NEVADA
48 46 44

ONE DAY, WHEN OUR SON was 11 months old, our three-year-old daughter left her puzzle on the floor. I told her, "If you leave it there, he'll eat it!" She didn't pick it up. Later, we walked by the room and he was putting together the last piece of the puzzle. We couldn't believe it. Mean parents that we were, we dumped it and made him do it again. And he did! Our son is off the charts now in math and science. He'll probably be an engineer.

—*CHERYL NORTON*
WASHOUGAL, WASHINGTON
13 11

EVEN BEFORE MY DAUGHTERS were old enough to understand what I was saying, I started reading to them. We had a great bedtime routine: I would give them their bottles, then their baths, and then I'd rock them in the rocking chair and read. Now, both of my daughters are reading on their own, and they love it!

—DONNA
ALLENTOWN, PENNSYLVANIA
7 6

INFANT INFO

When asked which comforting ritual was the hardest to break, 38 percent of parents said giving baby pacifier, 35 percent said rocking baby to sleep, 12 percent chose soothing baby with food, and 15 percent admitted all of the above.

INTERACT WITH YOUR BABY BY SINGING, reading, and talking to them on a daily basis. It's a proven fact that these things help babies with their language development. I'll sometimes talk to my daughter about my day at work. True, she won't understand much of what I'm saying, but she'll soon come to realize that words have meaning.

—EDWARD BARINQUE
EWA BEACH, HAWAII
7M

BABIES LOVE YOGA. Even before they're old enough to do it themselves, they love watching their moms do it—all the stretching and moving is interesting to them. I teach Mommy/Baby yoga classes, and I think babies can absorb some good habits about breathing and stretching and caring for body and spirit by starting yoga early.

—ELISE COLLINS
SAN FRANCISCO, CALIFORNIA
5

HAPPY FIRST BIRTHDAY!

THE FIRST BIRTHDAY PARTY is more for the parents than the child. The fun really starts at the second birthday.

—LYNDA DIFRANCESCO
RALEIGH, NORTH CAROLINA
2 2M

• • • • • • • •

IT IS BEST TO LIMIT THE NUMBER of guests so that baby doesn't get frightened or overwhelmed by large amounts of people. I would also suggest that you keep the guest list to familiar faces. Baby will be much more comfy if he or she knows most of the people swarming him or her.

—ERIN CALLAHAN
KERSHAW, SOUTH CAROLINA
2

• • • • • • • •

I WAS ACTUALLY VERY BLUE on my son's first birthday because he seemed to be growing so fast!

—D.
COLUMBUS, OHIO
7 4M

WE HAD A HUGE FIRST BIRTHDAY for our first son, because we thought he was a miracle, since we thought we couldn't have any children. Then, miracle two came along. His party will be big (because we want to be fair), but not as big.

—MICHELLE M.
OOSTBURG, WISCONSIN
2 2M

• • • • • • • •

SMALL FAMILY GATHERINGS WORK GREAT for first birthdays. For both of my daughters' first birthdays, I made each their own small chocolate cake and I just let them go to town. Boy, did they love that! Just simple, fun celebrations with close relatives, lots of balloons, and lots of photos.

—TINA SMITH
FORT COLLINS, COLORADO
4 2

• • • • • • • •

WHEN PLANNING A FIRST BIRTHDAY PARTY, delegate jobs. Have someone in charge of picking up the cake, helping with food, taking pictures, etc. You want to enjoy the party and not run around the whole time.

—BRYNN CYNOR
BUFFALO GROVE, ILLINOIS
1

IF YOU WANT THAT SPECIAL FIRST BIRTHDAY photo, my advice is to keep the cake with the burning candle out of reach of your kid. For my daughter's first birthday we had a little birthday cake with one candle on it. We thought it was so cute, and apparently, so did she, because as soon as we'd lit the candle and stepped back to take a picture, she stuck her hand right into the center of the flame and burned two fingers. Our first birthday picture of our daughter shows her with this shrieking look of pain on her face!

—DAVID BERNKNOPF
ATLANTA, GEORGIA
10 8

• • • • • • • •

CHILDREN ARE INHERENTLY CREATIVE and that creativity requires an environment that adapts to them and their explorations and experiments—even if they are very messy.

—SARAH COX
PORTLAND, MAINE
- 5 1

14 Discipline: Laying Down the Law

Sure, your baby is the cutest kid ever created. But that doesn't mean they're allowed to yank on puppy's ear or punch playmates in the nose. Discipline is in order, but what kind? The rules keep changing. Read on for tips on creating your very own little model citizen—during their first year, and beyond.

PARENTS NEED TO BE FLEXIBLE. Let kids stay up late sometimes. Enjoy life! Don't be rigid. Look at so many second kids—they are so much more flexible and easygoing then first kids because their parents aren't so uptight.

—*RONIT*
DENVER, COLORADO
3 1

RESPECT YOUR CHILD THE SAME WAY YOU WANT TO BE RESPECTED.

—*JUDITH WONG*
MILWAUKEE, WISCONSIN
5 2 4M

WHEN DISCIPLINING A BABY, reiterate the next morning everything you've told them the day before. They never remember and you're constantly reprogramming them. I said "no" many times, as a consequence, my daughter's first word was "no."

—*BONNIE L.*
CHICAGO, ILLINOIS
23 20

Find your own style of discipline and be consistent. Kids crave boundaries.

—*BONNIE ROBINDER*
LEANDER, TEXAS
17 13 9

• • • • • • • •

YOU ARE THE PARENT, YOU'RE IN CHARGE—you set the rules, limits and guidelines. It makes the child's life happier. When my son does something wrong, he gets a "bee"—a "time-out." He has a mobile in his room shaped like a bee that plays music for three minutes. Those three minutes allow him to reflect. It's about setting expectations—for example, after playing with his toys, he needs to pick them up and put them in the bin. Basic things. He's a kind, caring and independent child because we teach him consideration about actions and consequences.

—*MELISSA STEIN*
3

• • • • • • • •

WE USE TIMEOUT. It starts at five minutes for our two-year-old and 10 minutes for our four-year-old. If they continue to need disciplining, they sit there longer. If they are good, they can get out a little early. When it's over, we talk about why they were in timeout. If any apologies need to be made, those happen before they are allowed to go play. It has worked wonderfully so far!

—*JESSICA L. DELANEY*
JOHNSTOWN, COLORADO
4 2

THE OTHER OPTION: "YES"

I think some parents over-discipline. They just automatically say "no" to everything, even when there's really no reason for it. One day, for example, we were outside my husband's office. It's beautifully landscaped, with one of those dancing fountain things—the kind where beams of water suddenly come up and then disappear again. We were just enjoying looking at it and then suddenly there was my daughter and a friend in the middle of the beams of water. We quickly became the "enemy of the people" as other parents standing around would not allow their children to get wet.

But it was a warm day and I always carried extra clothes in the car. And, after all, once she was wet, what would have been accomplished by dragging her out? I don't mean to imply that we let her do everything; in fact, I've been accused more than once of being overprotective. I've just always looked for ways to say "yes" under appropriate conditions, not to automatically say "no."

—*Kathleen Jun Magyar*
Dallas, Texas
18

THE FIRST WORD MOST BABIES LEARN to understand is "no." But I believe the first word you should teach your child is actually "stop." More important than "no," the word "stop" is critical if you need to keep a little one from throwing a toy into a toilet, to prevent a baby from touching a stove, or to keep a toddler from running into the street.

—T.D.
IRON CITY, TENNESSEE
8 6 5

"Teach your children respect. It's a very big word."

—MICHELLE HIRSCH
ATLANTA, GEORGIA
8

I LIKE TO SIT THEM DOWN AND EXPLAIN things to them. I know they don't understand half of what I say, but they see that I take the time to sit with them and explain things to them in a calm voice. They listen really well, and they respect boundaries.

—FORREST
WELLINGTON, COLORADO
3 2

MY KIDS ARE SO AWESOME, and I couldn't possibly love them any more than I do, but there still are those days when I wish I could just take a break, leave them in the house, and get on a plane to Borneo for a week!

—JOHN SEYER
LOVELAND, COLORADO
3 1

FOR SAFETY'S SAKE I'VE INSISTED THAT MY SON sit on his bottom in the tub. If he tries to stand, I give him one "on your bottom" warning. If he doesn't immediately sit down, I get him right out of the bath, washed or not. Within a month, he had learned, and he's still really good about not standing in the tub. The other bath time rule is no throwing toys out of the tub. If he threw a toy out, I'd simply take it way. That ended that game pretty quickly!

—*JON*
BIGLERVILLE, PENNSYLVANIA
1

YOU HAVE TO REMEMBER THE PARENT AND CHILD roles, and milestones in the child's life are a real reminder. For example, at one year I had heard that you should stop giving a baby a bottle. So at the one-year check-up, I asked my doctor and he agreed, so I put all the bottles away. Some mothers hate to upset their children, so they continue to feed through a bottle. I gave my son a cup, which taught him independence.

—*MELISSA STEIN*
3

AS SOON AS OUR CHILDREN WERE OLD ENOUGH to leave the house, we took them everywhere with us, particularly out to dinner. It's important for them to learn how to act respectful in public as soon as possible. No matter how young they were, if my son was misbehaving in public, I'd pat him on his little ass. If my daughter was causing problems, I'd give her a very stern look. Eventually, they got the message.

—*ROBERT HARRIS*
LOS ANGELES, CALIFORNIA
26 17

If I ran out of patience, I'd find someone to watch my kids for 15 minutes. About 15 minutes was all I needed to regroup and not lose my temper.

—*DENICE W.*
WINDSOR, COLORADO
13 8

SPARE THE ROD?

NEVER SPANK A KID, ESPECIALLY A BABY. There are so many studies out that show how it actually ends up making kids more violent and have more behavior problems if they've been spanked. And especially for a baby, who is physically too young for his behavior to be "trained" in this way, it does nothing but erode the bond between parent and child. I have never hit my kids, and they are decent, well-behaved people.

—J.B.
SAN FRANCISCO, CALIFORNIA
15 12

• • • • • • • •

I DON'T BELIEVE IN SPANKING AS A FORM OF DISCIPLINE; instead we use timeouts—and not just for the kids, but for the parents, too. If ever I'm feeling like I want to yell at the boys, I step away for a minute. It helps me gather my composure. Plus, they usually say the sweetest things that it's hard to stay mad for very long anyway.

—HEATHER C.
EL CAJON, CALIFORNIA
4 2

• • • • • • • •

I PREFER TIMEOUTS AS A FORM OF DISCIPLINE, but for really nasty things (biting, spitting) I have resorted to spanking, though I really don't like to.

—TONYA LEE
MOUNT AIRY, MARYLAND
8 5

• • • • • • • •

PEOPLE HAVE STRONG FEELINGS EITHER WAY ABOUT SPANKING. I believe in it: not to hurt the kids, of course, but to make them look up. It hurts their little self esteem and gets their attention.

—BETTY
LOWER SAUCON, PENNSYLVANIA
34

We tried to spank my younger son when he misbehaved, but he had a diaper. So, he'd never even know we spanked him. He'd think it was being playful and funny. He'd double down and stick his bottom up and be more rambunctious. So now I take my little finger and I swat him right between the eyes. It doesn't leave a mark, or really hurt, but it gets his attention.

—E.
Eden Prairie, Minnesota
5 3

• • • • • • • •

I didn't spank my daughter when she was a baby, or ever. If she was acting up in the store, I took her home. Right then. You just have to remove them from the situation.

—B.J.
Wichita, Kansas
34

• • • • • • • •

Children under two are too young to be spanked on their bottoms. I don't think they really understand at that age. If our children were doing something really dangerous—like playing with an electrical outlet—we would lightly smack them on the hand and say, "No!" It startled them, and they got the message.

—Kristi Graham
Charlotte, North Carolina
4 1

WITH MY SECOND CHILD, I'm much more relaxed in my parenting approach. With your first child, you think, "Yikes, he's going to break a bone doing that." You don't have the time to worry when you have a second child. The second child seems to simply find their way . . . but I really don't know if it's temperament, birth order, or nature vs. nurture.

—*DIANA NAKANO*
SANTA CLARA, CALIFORNIA
5 3

"Use 'no' sparingly. We say 'no' only when it's serious. Otherwise, it loses its meaning."

—*BETHANY*
FORT COLLINS, COLORADO
11M

DON'T BE AFRAID TO LEAVE A GROCERY CART at the checkout and take your child out of the store if he's throwing a temper tantrum. If you have a screaming one-year-old, the store won't care if you're leaving.

—*CHERYL N.*
WASHOUGAL, WASHINGTON
13 11

MY DAUGHTER WAS NINE MONTHS OLD, barely starting to walk, and we were going on vacation. As we were packing, we saw that she kept going to the dog's food dish. We took her away from the dish. She didn't fuss. Well, she had a one-piece suit on with huge pockets. She had filled her pockets with dog food. She knew we were going to take her away from the dog food so she created a stash. We finally realized it, and emptied her pockets. Now, *that* made her furious.

—*CHERYL N.*
WASHOUGAL, WASHINGTON
13 11

LEARN TO BE FORGIVING AND ACCEPTING of your children—kids make mistakes. It's how they learn, and we are their teacher, not the critical person delivering punishment every time they are in error. Unconditional love grows beautiful children.

—*MAUREEN CALLAHAN*
CARMEL, INDIANA
16 12

INSTEAD OF PUTTING TIRED, CRABBY, NAUGHTY, two-year-old boys to bed, my husband put them in time out: one in the kitchen on a chair and the other in another room. The one on the kitchen chair fell asleep inside of three minutes, fell off and cut his forehead. He needed three stitches. Not everyone knows that time out is supposed to be one minute per year of age.

—*SHIRLEY GUTKOWSKI*
SUN PRAIRIE, WISCONSIN
26 25 -23 21

INFANT INFO

Discipline techniques that belittle or shame a child are truly harmful to development. Instead, show respect for your child's feelings and thoughts, while standing firm on your expectations for good behavior.

POTTY TRAINING TRICKS

SOMETIMES THE SECRET IS FINDING the right motivator. My oldest daughter was taking forever to potty train. But she desperately wanted to go to school. When she was around two, she'd stand at the window of our apartment each morning, watching as the much-older kids waited for the bus. One morning in frustration, I told her that she couldn't go to school until she was out of diapers. That day, she potty trained herself.

—*MARY BRIGHT*
ALLENTOWN, PENNSYLVANIA
33 31

• • • • • • • •

TO POTTY TRAIN MY SON, I bought rubber pants instead of those diaper-like training pants. With rubber pants, he can feel the mess, and he doesn't like it. It gives him incentive to use the toilet and not have accidents.

—*TAMARA SEYER*
LOVELAND, COLORADO

• • • • • • • •

THERE IS NO PERFECT WAY TO POTTY TRAIN. There will be accidents. There will be wet and poopy pants to change. So just take off the diapers and plunge in!

—*MARTY*
CHICAGO, ILLINOIS
17 15

• • • • • • • •

POTTY TRAIN THEM AS QUICKLY AS POSSIBLE. Not having to buy diapers is like getting a raise.

—*ANTHONY MANUEL*
KINDER, LOUISIANA
17 14 11

For toilet training, buy your baby underwear, but be prepared to do a lot of cleaning. Children love wearing underwear. My kids didn't like having accidents while wearing them and that made the toilet training go a little bit faster.

—D. Contreras-Garcez
Helotes, Texas
23 19 16 10

• • • • • • • •

Don't make potty training a battle, but do start the process before the kid is three years old. The habit was just so ingrained by then, we had a devil of a time getting our first to stop playing and go to the bathroom. By three, he just didn't mind sitting in a dirty diaper at all, as long as he could keep playing.

—A.L.
Boston, Massachusetts
6 4

• • • • • • • •

I potty trained my kids with M&Ms. If they went potty in the toilet, I would reward them with an M&M. This was the easiest method because I never gave my kids candy, so M&Ms were a big treat to them.

—Bonnie L.
Chicago, Illinois
23 20

WE ALWAYS SUPPLIED QUIET GAMES or art materials to keep our daughter occupied when we were out in public and she needed to stay still for a while. She turned out to be a sweet, appealing and well-behaved kid, so she basically went anywhere we went that was appropriate for a child.

—KATHLEEN JUN MAGYAR
DALLAS, TEXAS
18

• • • • • • • •

THERE IS NO GOOD WAY TO DISCIPLINE a child. Children turn out the way they turn out in spite of good or bad parenting.

—SHIRLEY GUTKOWSKI
SUN PRAIRIE, WISCONSIN
26 25 -23 21

• • • • • • • •

KIDS REQUIRE PREDICTABILITY in a schedule but also enough flexibility to change it as needed. So make a plan, but also have plans B, C, and D ready!

—ANDREA LARSON
FORT COLLINS, COLORADO
12 9

15

More Wisdom: Good Stuff That Doesn't Fit Anywhere Else

The most important thing to remember as you travel down the winding road of child rearing is that parenting is not a sprint, and it's not a marathon either—it's a lifelong journey. It helps to keep perspective on it all—to laugh and appreciate the toughest, most rewarding job ever created. As you read our final chapter on how to survive your baby, remember that one day, years from now, this will all be far behind you, and your baby might have his or her own kids . . . and at that point might even ask you for a bit of parenting advice. Good luck!

HAVING KIDS IS THE MOST AMAZING, scary, frustrating, wonderful, huge love that you're ever going to go through for the rest of your life.

—*K.J.*
ST. AUGUSTINE, FLORIDA
6 1

KISS YOUR BABIES A TON. THEY WILL GROW UP TO BE AFFECTIONATE!

—*STEPH D.*
BALTIMORE, MARYLAND
18 15 13

TO DRIVE A CAR, YOU NEED A LICENSE, and you need a permit to go fishing or to own a gun. But with children, there are no manuals. Raising children is truly life's greatest responsibility, but the approach is all trial and error.

—*PAULA FISCHER*
SAN JOSE, CALIFORNIA
13 12 6

Love them a lot. Just love them all the time and that's pretty much it.

—*TERI*
SEATTLE, WASHINGTON
12 8

I HAVE HAD FIVE KIDS. When you have more than one, you realize that the stages you thought would never end actually will. The first time around, you think your kid will never sleep through the night or ever be potty trained. But by the fifth kid, you know the stages of development well. So I would advise new parents to study the stages of development and realize that all things will pass. This will minimize panic and allow you to relax more.

—*A.M.*
PASSAIC, NEW JERSEY
12 10 8 6 3

KIDS CHANGE CONSTANTLY, and their care needs do as well. When we raised our kids, of course, there were difficult times. But we always had faith that if we planted the right values, they would sprout. And they have.

—*S.S.*
PASSAIC, NEW JERSEY

KIDS REACT TO HOW YOU REACT. Stressed out parents equal a stressed child. I'm highly prepared with food, wipes, diapers, toys in the car. I have snacks in my purse, etc.—so that alleviates any panic from being ill-prepared.

—*MELISSA STEIN*
3

EVERYTHING THAT YOU CAN PUT INTO your children is an investment for the future, whether you know it or not. It will come back to you tenfold when they are adults.

—*BRIAN COY*
EL CAJON, CALIFORNIA
23 21

"One time we brought our son to the doctor with a complaint. I asked if we needed a prescription. The doctor said, 'Yes,' and wrote one. It read, 'Reassurance.' That's all we needed!"

—*DEANA KRAUSE*
CHICAGO, ILLINOIS
11 9

THE MORE TIME YOU GIVE THEM AS KIDS, the less time they'll spend in a shrink's office when they're older. Don't think that buying them presents is a substitute for being there with them—it's not. There is no real substitute for parents.

—*ANONYMOUS*
BETHESDA, MARYLAND
9 6

Sleep while you can. And carry Handi-Wipes.

—*JENNIFER LAWLER*
LAWRENCE, KANSAS
7

IT IS SO EASY TO GET CAUGHT up in everything that you need to do for baby on a daily basis—changing diapers, feeding, changing and washing clothes, getting them down for naps, etc.—that you can miss out on precious moments. Appreciate every second with the baby. They are only that age once. If the laundry piles up because you want to cuddle with the baby, then so be it.

—*BARB G.*
PITTSBURGH, PENNSYLVANIA
9 2

• • • • • • • •

WRITE A LETTER TO YOUR CHILD EVERY YEAR that tells them about all the important events that have gone on in their lives. This gives him or her a connection to family. I keep records of things like where we went on vacation, what my daughter's favorite toys were, and who was her boyfriend. I lost my mom when I was 14, and I don't know about a lot of my childhood. Writing a letter each year lets my children know how important they are to me.

—*S.F.*
SAN ANTONIO, TEXAS
20 16

Appreciate your babies all you can. They'll be terrible teenagers soon enough.

—*M.F.*
TUCSON, ARIZONA
35 33 31 30

• • • • • • • •

HOW DID I SURVIVE THE FIRST YEAR of being the single mother of twins? I was naïve. Being in this situation for the first time, I didn't know what to expect, so I didn't realize the enormous effort that I had made until long after I made it. I was so busy "doing" that there was no time to reflect, think about the future, etc. All I could do was deal with the moment.

—*NANCY LOU W.*
LITTLE SILVER, NEW JERSEY
-5

ALWAYS CARRY A PLASTIC BAG WITH YOU. You never know when you'll get a half-chewed graham cracker or dirty diaper that needs to be disposed of.

—*LORI B.*
CHARLESTON, SOUTH CAROLINA
19 16 13 3

NEW PARENTS ARE SO WRAPPED UP in "the first time my baby did this, the first time they did that, etc." But it's also important to remember that things will—and do—change. Try to think about "the last time my baby took a bottle" and "the last time my baby wore a diaper, slept in a crib, nursed, took a nap, etc." These are important milestones, too!

—*WENDY SNYDER*
WESTMINSTER, COLORADO
8 4

Don't have more than two kids. Once they have you outnumbered you're in trouble.

—*CINDY RODGERS*
PITTSBURGH, PENNSYLVANIA
17

"I think the idea of "surviving" your baby is flawed thinking. Babies are a gift from God, the most precious gift we get, and every moment with them should be cherished."

—*DIANE SMITH*
HARMONY, PENNSYLVANIA
20 19 17 16 15

THE TAO OF PARENTHOOD

I spent a large part of my 20s searching for spiritual truth, awakening, maybe enlightenment even. I learned to meditate, practice yoga, demand discipline and honor respect. But nothing compares to the daily spiritual practice that I experience with my children. You've heard it before—children are our best teachers. Well, I have three wild, funny, lovable Buddhas who teach me everyday. If you think you know what your children need, well, you're missing the great opportunity. The real lesson is not about how you will discipline them, get them to eat their vegetables or stay in their bed at night. The real lesson is in letting go of the chaos of motherhood—finding your true self, your inner calm, when life is swirling by you.

At the park the other day I was holding conversations with two different mothers, pushing my seven-month-old in her stroller while chasing my two-year-old so I could change his poopy diaper, and keeping an eye out for my three-year-old who had run off in another direction to look for a caterpillar he named Bobby. No, I don't have time these days to be searching for enlightenment in lotus atop a mountain, but I don't really have the need to, either. I have just what I need to make me a better person right here in front of me.

—Julie Warner Miccichi
Atlanta, Georgia
4 2 7M

LET THEM RUN AROUND WITH DIFFERENT-COLORED shoes, or no shoes at all. It's OK if they wear clothes that don't match. I just let my two-year-old enjoy being a little girl.

—SHARI LONG, CNM (MIDWIFE)
CHEYENNE, WYOMING
21 19 12 2

Love them and hold them and believe that you can't spoil them. You just have to keep them warm and safe and fed.

—DEB S.
EL CAJON, CALIFORNIA
22 13

I WAS NERVOUS ABOUT EVERYTHING when my first child was born. When my husband and I brought her home from the hospital, I held a tissue up to her nose so she wouldn't breathe in any germs! When I had my son nine-and-a-half years later, it was completely different. When we left the hospital with him, we stopped at McDonald's on the way home! But the good news is that even with these two completely different parenting styles, both of my kids are terrific adults, with successful lives of their own.

—ANONYMOUS
LONG VALLEY, NEW JERSEY
32 23

MY BIGGEST SURPRISE about having a baby? Realizing how much I could love someone. Perhaps that sounds corny. But for me, every day was like Christmas with my baby son. I jumped out of bed excited about spending another day with him. I held him for almost the entire first year of his life. That amount of love is overwhelming. No, the feeling does not end. He's 34 now and we're still very close.

—NAN B.
WILLIAMSBURG, VIRGINIA
34

THE THING I WOULD DO DIFFERENTLY if I had it all to do over: I wouldn't worry so much about the mess kids make when they are young. I used to run myself ragged picking up after them constantly. Now I'd just let it be. Who cares?

—*CHARLENE DEPASQULE*
PITTSBURGH, PENNSYLVANIA
21 18 15

"Babies make you younger and older at the same time—younger because you care for them and see things through a child's eyes, and older because you must become more mature and less selfish."

—*JENNIFER B.*
YARDLEY, PENNSYLVANIA

Babies arrive with personalities. Get to know yours.

—*MELODY PHILLIPS*
SARATOGA SPRINGS, NEW YORK
17 16

HOLD YOUR CHILDREN A LOT. I've seen the merits of it particularly with my four-year-old granddaughter. She's always been held and hugged a lot, and she's a very happy, social child. Parents used to be told, "Don't hold your children so much, you'll spoil them." That is not true. You can never hold them and love them enough.

—*JOYCE*
FORT COLLINS, COLORADO
31 29 25 20

IF YOU HAVE A BICULTURAL KID, it's important to keep them connected with both cultures. I think that's especially true if they're biracial, as they will most definitely go through periods where they identify more with one race or the other. Our son considers himself both a white American and Filipino-American, and he knows a lot about both cultures.

—*JULIE*
SAN FRANCISCO, CALIFORNIA
13

Keep hand and foot prints of your newborn. You'll never believe they were once that small!

—*ANONYMOUS*
17 14

JUST LOVE THEM. Everything else comes along and falls into place. They get potty trained. They give up their bottle. In the grand scheme of things, these "milestones" really aren't so important. They happen when they happen. Each child is different, so you have to figure out what each one needs, and then you have to do it. If they need a pacifier or a blanket, let them have it. They'll outgrow these things on their own, in their own time. My daughter gave up her bottle when she was 13 months old. My son had his bottle until he was four years old. Big deal! Now they're both well-adjusted adults. I learned to be flexible when it comes to growth and development.

—*ANONYMOUS*
FORT COLLINS, COLORADO
25 18

TEACH YOUR CHILDREN TO BE PASSIONATE when they're little—whether it's about you, a favorite toy, or the movie you've watched a thousand times. When they grow up, that passion will guide them. Support the journey!

—*MARY M.*
SPRINGFIELD, ILLINOIS
21 17

DADS, IF YOU'RE GOING TO SHAVE off facial hair, do it just a little bit day by day, and let the baby watch you. My eight-month-old daughter screamed the first time she saw me after I shaved off my beard. She cried every time she looked at me for days and was terrified of me.

—JACK MORRIS
BOSTON, MASSACHUSETTS
42 41 36

Hug your child at every opportunity and always talk to them in a soothing voice.

—K.K.
FALMOUTH, MAINE
32 29

AS THE PARENT OF A DISABLED CHILD, the best advice I have for any parent is to be the author of your own expectations. Don't let other people's expectations become yours. No one else can possibly know what my life is like, so their opinions and judgments are absolutely immaterial to me. It's very refreshing for someone who spent too much of her life worrying about what other people think.

—JENNIFER LAWLER
LAWRENCE, KANSAS
6

ANYBODY WHO HAS BEEN THROUGH PARENTING has probably learned something that could come in handy to you. Don't dismiss any advice outright.

But at the same time everybody has a different idea of how to raise their babies and you may not want to do something just because it worked for someone else. Don't be afraid to try something that you wouldn't ordinarily. You may be pleasantly surprised!

—C.M.
PITTSBURGH, PENNSYLVANIA
19 17

WORDS TO LIVE BY

When it comes to parenting, the only thing you truly have control over is yourself. Really. You might think you can read a baby book and find a solution to why your three-month-old isn't sleeping through the night like your neighbor's child, but most likely you'll just be disappointed. And we all would like to think that all of our daily efforts will produce the most well-adjusted, caring, responsible 18-year-old who will make honor roll her freshmen year at an Ivy League college while volunteering on weekends to serve soup to the homeless. Que sera sera—whatever will be will be. If you want to give your children a real gift, be true to yourself. Work on becoming the best person you can be. When your children look into the eyes of a confident, powerful and happy human being, they'll know that it is attainable to them.

—*Julie Warner Miccichi*
Atlanta, Georgia
4 2 7M

If someone offers help, take it!

—*Laura Kronen*
New York, New York
15M

Don't miss a thing. Not the first tooth, not the first steps. That is my biggest regret— that I had to work too much. It means a lot for kids to have their parents around. Even if you have to live in a smaller apartment, or never eat out, or share a car: One of you shouldn't work full-time during the early years. You can always go back to a job when they start school.

—*Jane Powell*
Earlysville, Virginia
34 31

"Don't stress yourself about a clean house and clean children. They can mess it up faster than you can pick it up."

—*Mary Beckering*
Syracuse, New York
5 3

My favorite piece of parenting advice came from my mother. When I was pregnant, my mother said, "No matter how hard any parenting stage is, it will always pass. Nothing will last forever." It's so true: Messy eating, diaper changing, and colds and stomach bugs don't last forever. In a few days, weeks, or months each of them will pass. Keeping this advice in mind really helps you get through the tough spots.

—*Paula*
Northampton, Pennsylvania
3 1

My mother, who's still alive at 96, says that a baby should always be wearing a hat to keep it warm. Well, don't let my mother see you, but I think it's OK if the baby is not always covered. They're not that fragile.

—*Mary C.*
Tucson, Arizona
35 33 31 30

You're not going to get everything done on your to-do list—no, the housekeeping won't all get done. At least you vacuumed today; good for you. Now make time to get down on the floor and play with your children. It goes by fast. Make the decision to enjoy your children.

—*Tori Koppelmaa*
San Jose, California
6 - 4 2

Hug and kiss your kids a lot. Even if you're not normally a hugger, it will eventually feel natural, and it helps you raise really happy kids.

—*S.M.P.*
Portland, Maine
12 8

Parenthood can bring out the best and the worst in you. You have to re-evaluate a lot of things in your life, and you summon this reserve of patience you never entirely knew existed. All of your issues from your own parents come up, and after all the analysis and acknowledging that you want to do a better job than your own parents, you may, ironically, end up parenting like them.

—*Paula Fischer*
San Jose, California
13 12 6

Babies heighten your senses—sight, touch, hearing and smell. Especially hearing and smell.

—*Helen Bradt*
Laurel, Maryland
33 30 28 25

READY FOR COLLEGE?

START YOUR COLLEGE FUND EARLY. Compound interest makes it better to save $20 a month from the time your kid is one day old than to save $100 a month starting when they're five. And, there's no such thing as too small an amount. Even if at the end of the year you only have $60, that's still $60.

—*ROB MCHARGUE*
SAN ANTONIO, TEXAS
12 11

• • • • • • • • •

I WAS NEVER A COUPON CLIPPER, BUT NOW THAT I HAVE KIDS, I save an incredible amount of money with coupons. I save more than $30 a week on groceries. The other day I got $15 in rebate checks for buying just three cans of baby formula. I also shop yard sales, which I never did before having kids.

—*SARAH SISSON CHRISTENSEN*
SAN DIEGO, CALIFORNIA
2 2M

• • • • • • • • •

MY WIFE AND I WOULD THINK NOTHING of having a four dollar coffee every day but somehow couldn't find any leftover money for college savings. So, we've stopped coffee cold turkey and put eight dollars per day (actually $250 per month) toward her college savings. If we continue for the next 17 years or so, she should have enough to pay for three to four years of a public college or about half of a private college.

—*CARL*
MINNEAPOLIS, MINNESOTA
1

SET UP A COLLEGE ACCOUNT FOR A NEW BABY as soon as you possibly can. Start early and save, save, save.

—*S.M.P.*
PORTLAND, MAINE
12 8

• • • • • • • •

CHECK IF YOUR EMPLOYER OFFERS A CHILDCARE FLEX ACCOUNT. It allows you to take out pre-tax money from your check for childcare. That saves money, especially when you have more than one child.

—*KRISTI GRAHAM*
CHARLOTTE, NORTH CAROLINA
4 1

• • • • • • • •

IF NOTHING ELSE STICKS, KNOW THIS: PAY YOURSELF FIRST. Put aside one hour's pay a day, and don't touch it, ever.

—*SHIRLEY GUTKOWSKI*
SUN PRAIRIE, WISCONSIN
26 25 -23 21

• • • • • • • •

SHOP AT CONSIGNMENT AND RE-SALE SHOPS TO SAVE MONEY. They're better than garage sales because they check for stains, stuck zippers, and missing buttons before accepting something to sell. As your babies outgrow their clothes, sell their old clothes and buy new ones at consignment stores.

—*KIRSTEN*
FORT COLLINS, COLORADO
6 3

• • • • • • • •

SAVE NOW, or pay later.

—*JWAIII*
ATLANTA, GEORGIA
5 2

WHEN YOU'RE A PARENT WITH YOUNG KIDS, you're so busy earning a living, making a home, and raising your kids that you don't have even one second to enjoy those moments. But when you're older, with a little distance, you realize that the brief time your kids are babies is precious.

—*ANONYMOUS*
LONG VALLEY, NEW JERSEY
32 23

I THINK A LOT OF PEOPLE WORRY when they're having a second baby that they couldn't possibly love the second baby as much as they do their first. I know I worried about that. Your first baby is the center of your life. You worry that your second baby will be an interruption. But the amazing thing is, you do love that second baby every single bit as much as the first.

—*W.F.*
MERTZTOWN, PENNSYLVANIA
24 20

FOCUS ON YOUR RELATIONSHIP with your spouse or partner as much as or more than you focus on your relationship with your child. Children who live with happy grown-ups who express love for one another learn to be happy children who express love for one another. I read that what a child needs most is a cheerful care provider. I really think this is true.

—*S.C.*
PORTLAND, MAINE
-5 1

THIS IS NOT A TEST. Don't get so caught up in trying to be so perfect that you don't enjoy your baby.

—*MELODY PHILLIPS*
SARATOGA SPRINGS, NEW YORK
17 16

CREDITS

Page 20: ABC News.

Page 35: Discovery Channel Health Series.

Page 41: Social Security Administration, 2003.

Page 43: Social Security Administration, 2003.

Page 49: Cheryl Perlitz, author of *Soaring Through Setbacks.*

Page 54: *Family Fun* Magazine, 2004.

Page 69: Brigitte Thompson, www.DaycareRecordkeeping.com.

Page 76: Reuters Health, Charnicia E. Huggins, September 14, 2004.

Page 89: www.todaysmom.com.

Page 100: www.todaysmom.com.

Page 107: *Family Fun* Magazine, 2004.

Page 113: "Poll Finds Even Babies Don't Get Enough Rest," by David Tuller, *New York Times*, March 30, 2004.

Page 118: W. Bruce Cameron, Nationally syndicated columnist and author of *8 Simple Rules for Dating My Teenage Daughter* and *How to Remodel a Man.*

Page 136: "Vital Signs: Behavior; A Warm Welcome to the World," by John O'Neil, New York Times, April 13, 2004.

Page 147: The Associated Press, June 17, 2003.

Page 157: Brette Sember, author of the upcoming book *Practical Pregnancy: A Month by Month Legal and Practical Guide for New and Expectant Parents.*

Page 168: Elaine Fantle Shimberg, author of 20 books including *Blending Families* and *Another Chance for Love, Finding a Partner Later in Life.*

Page 185: American Academy of Allergy, Asthma and Immunology.

Page 202: *The Late Talker: What to Do if Your Child Isn't Talking Yet*, by Dr. Marilyn C. Agin, Lisa F. Geng and Malcolm J. Nicholl.

Page 207: *Parenting* Magazine, October 2004.

Page 219: www.About.com.

HELP YOUR FRIENDS SURVIVE!

Order extra copies of *How to Survive Your Baby's First Year.*

Check your local bookstore or order here.

Please send me ______ copies of *How to Survive Your Baby's First Year.*

Enclose $12.95 for each copy. Add $4.00 for shipping and handling for one book, and $2.00 for each additional book. Georgia residents must include applicable sales tax. Payment must accompany orders. Please allow 3 weeks for delivery.

My check for $__________ is enclosed.
Please charge my __ Visa __ MasterCard __ American Express

Name ____

Organization ______________________________________

Address ____

City/State/Zip _____________________________________

Phone ______________________ Email _________________

Credit card # ______________________________________

Exp. Date _____________ Signature ___________________

Please make checks payable to Hundreds of Heads Books, Inc.

Please fax to 212-937-2220, or mail to:

HUNDREDS OF HEADS BOOKS, INC.
#230
2221 Peachtree Road, Suite D
Atlanta, Georgia 30309

HELP WRITE THE NEXT Hundreds of Heads™ SURVIVAL GUIDE!

*Tell us your story about a life experience, and what lesson you learned from it. If we use your story in one of our books, we'll send you a free copy. Use this card or visit **www.hundredsofheads.com** (indicate 'referred by BRC').*

Here's my story/advice on surviving

❑ **DATING** ❑ **MARRIAGE** (years married: ________)

❑ **FRESHMAN YEAR** (college and year of graduation: ____________________)

❑ **A NEW JOB** (years working:______ profession/job:____________________)

❑ **A MOVE** (# of times you've moved:____) ❑ **A DIET** (# of lbs. lost in best diet: ____)

❑ **A TEENAGER** (ages/sexes of your children:__________________________)

❑ **DIVORCE** (times married: _______ times divorced:_______)

❑ ___________________________ **OTHER TOPIC** (you pick)

Name: ______________________________City/State: ______________________

❑ Use my name ❑ Use my initials only ❑ Anonymous

(Note: Your entry in the book may also include city/state and the descriptive information above.)

How should we contact you *(this will not be published or shared):*

email: ____________________________ other: ___________________________

Please mail to:

HUNDREDS OF HEADS BOOKS, INC.
#230
2221 Peachtree Road, Suite D
Atlanta, Georgia 30309

Waiver: All entries are property of Hundreds of Heads Books, Inc., and may be edited, published in any medium, etc. By submitting content, you grant Hundreds of Heads Books, Inc. and its affiliates a royalty-free, perpetual, irrevocable, non-exclusive right (including any moral rights) and license to use, reproduce, modify, adapt, publish, translate, create derivative works from, distribute, communicate to the public, perform and display the content (in whole or in part) worldwide and/or to incorporate it in other works in any form, media, or technology now known or later developed, for the full term of any Rights that may exist in such content, and to identify you (with the information above) as the contributor of content you submit.

Your story/advice:

ABOUT THE EDITORS

LORI BANOV KAUFMANN is a business consultant. She is the co-author of *The Boston Ice Cream Lover's Guide* and ate so much ice cream while researching that book that when she was pregnant she craved bagels with Muenster cheese instead of sweets. Lori has four great kids, all of whom were babies at one point. She holds an AB from Princeton University and an MBA from the Harvard Business School.

JAMIE ALLEN is an editor and "chief headhunter" for the HUNDREDS OF HEADS . . . survival guide series. He spent five years as a senior writer and editor with CNN.com, and his nonfiction work has appeared in numerous publications. He lives in Atlanta with his wife and two young children.

YADIN KAUFMANN is a founder of a venture capital firm that invests in high-technology start-up companies, some of which bear a strong resemblance to infants. (He also is responsible for those four great kids.) He received his AB from Princeton University, JD from Harvard Law School, and AM from Harvard's Graduate School of Arts and Sciences.

VISIT WWW.HUNDREDSOFHEADS.COM

Do you have something interesting to say about marriage, your in-laws, dieting, holding a job, or one of life's other challenges?

 Help humanity—share your story!

 Get published in our next book!

 Find out about the upcoming titles in the HUNDREDS OF HEADS™ survival guide series!

 Read up-to-the-minute advice on many of life's challenges!

 Sign up to become an interviewer for one of the next HUNDREDS OF HEADS™ survival guides!

Visit www.hundredsofheads.com today!

Other Books from HUNDREDS OF HEADS™ BOOKS

HOW TO SURVIVE YOUR FRESHMAN YEAR . . . by Hundreds of Sophomores, Juniors, and Seniors Who Did (and some things to avoid, from a few dropouts who didn't)™
(April 2004; ISBN 0-9746296-0-0)

HOW TO SURVIVE DATING . . . by Hundreds of Happy Singles Who Did (and some things to avoid, from a few broken hearts who didn't)™
(October 2004; ISBN 0-9746296-1-9)

HOW TO SURVIVE YOUR MARRIAGE . . . by Hundreds of Happy Couples Who Did (and some things to avoid, from a few divorcees who didn't)™
(February 2005; ISBN 0-9746296-4-3)

HOW TO SURVIVE YOUR TEENAGER . . . by Hundreds of Still-Sane Parents Who Did (and some things to avoid, from a few whose kids drove them nuts)™
(Spring 2005; ISBN 0-9746296-3-5)

HOW TO SURVIVE A MOVE . . . by Hundreds of Happy Dwellers Who Did (and some things to avoid, from a few who haven't upacked yet)™
(Spring 2005; 0-9746292-5-1)

HOW TO SURVIVE A DIVORCE . . . by Hundreds of Happy Exes Who Did (and some things to avoid, from a few who haven't gotten over it yet)™
(Spring 2005; 0-9746292-6-X)

HELP WRITE THE NEXT Hundreds of Heads™ SURVIVAL GUIDE!

*Tell us your story about a life experience, and what lesson you learned from it. If we use your story in one of our books, we'll send you a free copy. Use this card or visit **www.hundredsofheads.com** (indicate 'referred by BRC').*

Here's my story/advice on surviving

❑ **DATING** ❑ **FRESHMAN YEAR** (college and year of graduation: ______)
❑ **MARRIAGE** (years married: ____) ❑ **A NEW JOB** (years working:____ profession/job: ______)
❑ **YOUR BABY'S FIRST YEAR** (ages/sexes of your children:______)
❑ **A MOVE** (# of times you've moved:______) ❑ **DIVORCE** (times married:______ times divorced:______)
❑ **DIET** (# of lbs. you've lost in best diet: ______) ❑ ______ **OTHER TOPIC** (you pick)

Name: ______ City/State: ______

❑ Use my name ❑ Use my initials only ❑ Anonymous

(Your entry in the book may also include city/state and the descriptive information above.)

How should we contact you *(this will not be published or shared):*
email: ______ other: ______

Here's my story/advice: ______

need more room? visit www.hundredsofheads.com

Ref. ______

HELP WRITE THE NEXT Hundreds of Heads™ SURVIVAL GUIDE!

*Tell us your story about a life experience, and what lesson you learned from it. If we use your story in one of our books, we'll send you a free copy. Use this card or visit **www.hundredsofheads.com** (indicate 'referred by BRC').*

Here's my story/advice on surviving

❑ **DATING** ❑ **FRESHMAN YEAR** (college and year of graduation: ______)
❑ **MARRIAGE** (years married: ____) ❑ **A NEW JOB** (years working:____ profession/job: ______)
❑ **YOUR BABY'S FIRST YEAR** (ages/sexes of your children:______)
❑ **A MOVE** (# of times you've moved:______) ❑ **DIVORCE** (times married:______ times divorced:______)
❑ **DIET** (# of lbs. you've lost in best diet: ______) ❑ ______ **OTHER TOPIC** (you pick)

Name: ______ City/State: ______

❑ Use my name ❑ Use my initials only ❑ Anonymous

(Your entry in the book may also include city/state and the descriptive information above.)

How should we contact you *(this will not be published or shared):*
email: ______ other: ______

Here's my story/advice: ______

need more room? visit www.hundredsofheads.com

Waiver: All entries are property of Hundreds of Heads Books, Inc., and may be edited, published in any medium, etc. By submitting content, you grant Hundreds of Heads Books, Inc. and its affiliates a royalty-free, perpetual, irrevocable, non-exclusive right (including any moral rights) and license to use, reproduce, modify, adapt, publish, translate, create derivative works from, distribute, communicate to the public, perform and display the content (in whole or in part) worldwide and/or to incorporate it in other works in any form, media, or technology now known or later developed, for the full term of any Rights that may exist in such content, and to identify you (with the information above) as the contributor of content you submit.

Ref. ______

NO POSTAGE NECESSARY IF MAILED IN THE UNITED STATES

BUSINESS REPLY MAIL

FIRST-CLASS MAIL PERMIT NO. 220 ATLANTA, GA

POSTAGE WILL BE PAID BY ADDRESSEE

HUNDREDS OF HEADS BOOKS, INC.
#230
2221 Peachtree Road, Suite D
Atlanta, Georgia 30309

NO POSTAGE NECESSARY IF MAILED IN THE UNITED STATES

BUSINESS REPLY MAIL

FIRST-CLASS MAIL PERMIT NO. 220 ATLANTA, GA

POSTAGE WILL BE PAID BY ADDRESSEE

HUNDREDS OF HEADS BOOKS, INC.
#230
2221 Peachtree Road, Suite D
Atlanta, Georgia 30309

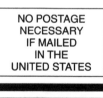